A
TREATISE

ON THE

SOCIAL COMPACT;

OR

The PRINCIPLES of

POLITIC LAW.

By J. J. ROUSSEAU,

Citizen of GENEVA.

——————— *Fœde is æquas*
Dicamus leges.   Æneid. xi.

LONDON:
Printed for T. BECKET and P. A. DE HONDT,
in the Strand.   MDCCLXIV.

ADVERTISEMENT.

THIS little treatife is taken from a much larger work, in which I formerly engaged, without having duly confulted my abilities. I have, therefore, long fince laid it afide; conceiving it proper to offer the following extract only to the public, as the leaft extionable part of the performance.

CONTENTS.

BOOK I.

In which the tranſition from a ſtate of nature to that of ſociety, is inveſtigated, with the eſſential conditions of the ſocial compaɛt.

CHAP.

CONTENTS.

CHAP. IV.

BOOK

CONTENTS.

BOOK II.

Concerning the Legislature.

CHAP.

CONTENTS.

CHAP. VII.

BOOK III.

Concerning political laws, or the forms of Government.

CHAP. I.

CHAP.

CONTENTS.

CHAP. II.

CHAP.

CONTENTS.

CHAP. IX.

CHAP. X.

CHAP. XI.

CHAP. XII.

CHAP. XIII.

CHAP. XIV.

CHAP. XV.

CHAP.

CONTENTS.

CHAP. XVI.

CHAP. XVII.

CHAP. XVIII.

BOOK IV.

In which the subject of political laws is continued, and the means of strengthening the constitution of the state considered.

CHAP. I.

CHAP. II.

CHAP.

CONTENTS.

CHAP. III.

CHAP. IV.

CHAP. V.

CHAP. VI.

CHAP. VII.

CHAP. VIII.

CHAP. IX.

A

A

T R E A T I S E

ON THE

SOCIAL COMPACT, &c.

BOOK I.

INTRODUCTION.

MY defign, in the prefent treatife, is to
inquire, Whether the nature of fociety
admits of any fixed and equitable rules of government, fuppofing mankind to be fuch as they
are, and their laws fuch as they might be made.
In this inveftigation I fhall endeavour conftantly
to join the confiderations of natural right and
public intereft, fo that juftice and utility may
never be difunited.

This being premifed, I fhall enter on my fubject, without expatiating on its importance. If
B   it

it be afked, Whether I am a prince or legiflator, that I thus take upon me to write on politics ? I anfwer, I am neither ; and that it is for
this reafon I write.   Were I a prince or legiflator I would not throw away my time in pointing
out what ought to be done ; I would myfelf put
it in practice, or be filent.

As the citizen of a free ftate, and a member
of the fupreme power, by birth, however weak
may be the influence of my fingle vote in public
affairs, the right of giving that vote is fufficient
to impofe on me the duty of making thofe affairs
my ftudy, thinking myfelf happy in difcuffing the
various forms of government, to find every day
new reafons for admiring that of my own country * !

C H A P. I.

The fubject of the firft book.

MAN is born free, and yet is univerfally
enflaved.   At the fame time, an individual frequently conceives himfelf to be the lord
and mafter over others, though only more emi-
nently deprived of liberty.   Whence can this
change arife ? Are there any means by which
it may be rendered lawful ? The former quef-

* Geneva.

tion

tion I cannot anfwer, though I imagine myfelf capable of refolving the latter.

If I took into confideration only the exiftence and effects of power, I fhould fay, So long as a people are compelled to obey, they do well to be obedient ; but, as foon as they are in a capacity to refift, they do better to throw off the yoke of reftraint : For, in recovering their liberty on the fame plea by which they loft it, either they have a juft right to reaffume it, or thofe could have none who deprived them of it. But there is an inviolable right founded on the very nature of fociety, which ferves as the bafis of all others. Man doth not derive this right, however, immediately from nature; it is founded on mutual convention. We muft proceed, then, to inquire, of what kind fuch convention muft have been. But, before we come to argue this point, I fhould eftablifh what I have already advanced.

CHAP. II.

On the primitive ftate of fociety.

THE moft ancient of all focieties, and the only natural one, is that of a family. And even in this, children are no longer connected with their father, than while they ftand in need of his affiftance. When this becomes

needlefs,

needlefs, the natural tie is of courfe diffolved,
the children are exempted from the obedience
they owe their father, and the father is equally fo
from the folicitude due from him to his children ;
both affume a ftate of independence refpecting
each other.   They may continue, indeed, to live
together afterwards ; but their connection, in
fuch a cafe, is no longer natural, but voluntary;
and even the family union is then maintained by
mutual convention.

This liberty, which is common to all mankind, is the neceffary confequence of our very
nature ; whofe firft law being that of felf-pre-
fervation, our principal concerns are thofe which
relate to ourfelves ; no fooner, therefore, doth
man arrive at years of difcretion, than he becomes the only proper judge of the means of that
prefervation, and of courfe his own mafter. ´

In a family, then, we may fee the firft model
of political focieties : their chief is reprefented
by the father, and the people by his children,
while all of them being free, and equal by birth,
they cannot alienate their liberty, but for their
common intereft. All the difference between a family and a ftate, lies in this, That, in the former,
the love which a father naturally bears to his
children is a compenfation for his folicitude concerning them ; and, in the latter, it is the pleafure

of

of command that fupplies the place of this love, which a chief doth not entertain for his people.

Grotius denies that government is invefted with power folely for the benefit of thofe who are governed, and cites the cafe of flaves as an example. It is, indeed, his conftant practice, to eftablifh the matter of right on the matter of fact *. He might have employed a more con-clufive method, though not a more favourable one for tyrannical governments.

It is then doubtful, according to Grotius, whether the whole race of mankind, except about an hundred individuals, belong to thofe individuals, or whether the latter belong to the whole race of mankind ; and he appears, throughout his whole work, to lean to the for-mer opinion. This is alfo the opinion of Hobbes. Thus they divide the human fpecies in-to herds of cattle, each of which hath its keeper, who protects it from others, only that he may make a property of it himfelf.

* " The learned refearches into the laws of nature and nations are often nothing more than the hiftory of ancient abufes ; fo that it is a ridiculous infatuation to be too fond of ftudying them." *Manufcript Trea-tife on the Interefts of France, by the Marquis d'A.* This was exactly the cafe with Grotius.

As

As a fhepherd is of a fuperior nature to his flock, fo the herd-keepers of men, or their chiefs, are of a fuperior nature to the herd, over which they prefide. Such was the reafoning, according to Philo, of the Emperor Caligula, who concluded logically enough from this ana-logy, that either kings were gods, or their fub-jects no better than brutes.

This argument of Caligula bears much refem-blance to thofe of Hobbes and Grotius. Arif-totle had faid, indeed, before either of them, that men were not naturally equal; but that fome of them were born to flavery, and others to dominion.

Ariftotle was right as to the fact, but miftook the effect for the caufe. Nothing is more cer-tain, than that every man born in flavery is born to be a flave. In fuch a ftate, men lofe even the defire of freedom, and prefer fubjection, as the companions of Ulyffes did their brutality *. If there are any flaves, therefore, by nature, it is becaufe they are flaves contrary to nature. Power firft made flaves, and cowardice hath per-petuated them.

* See a little tract written by Plutarch, on the ra-tionality of brutes.

I have

I have faid nothing of king Adam, or the emperor Noah, father of three monarchs, who, like the children of Saturn, as fome have imagined them to be, divided the world among them. I hope my moderation alfo in this refpect will be efteemed fome merit; for, as I am defcended in a right line from one of thefe princes, and probably from the eldeft branch of the family, how do I know, that, by a regular deduction of my defcent, I might not find myfelf the legitimate heir to univerfal monarchy? Be this, however, as it may, it cannot be denied, that Adam had as good a title to the fovereignty of the world, when he was the only perfon in it, as Robinfon Crufoe had to that of his ifland under the fame circumftances. A very great conveniency alfo attended their government, in that the monarch might reft fecurely on his throne, without fear of wars, confpiracies, or rebellion.

C H A P. III.

On the right of the Strongeſt.

THE ftrongeft is not ftrong enough to continue always mafter, unlefs he transforms his power into a right of command, and obedience into a duty. Hence is deduced the right of the ftrongeft; a right taken ironically in appearance,

pearance, and laid down as an eſtabliſhed principle in reality. But will this term never be
rightly explained ? Force, in the ſimpleſt ſenſe,
is a phyſical power ; nor can I ſee what morality
can reſult from its effeᶜts. To yield to ſuperior
force is an aᶜt of neceſſity, not of the will ; at
moſt it is but an aᶜt of prudence. And in what
ſenſe can this be called a duty ?

Let us ſuppoſe, however, for a moment, this
pretended right eſtabliſhed, and we ſhall ſee it
attended with inexplicable abſurdities ; for, if it
be admitted, that power conſtitutes right, the
effeᶜt changes with the cauſe, and every ſucceed-
ing power, if greater than the former, ſucceeds
alſo to the right ; ſo that men may lawfully diſ-
obey, as ſoon as they can do it, with impunity ;
and, as right is always on the ſtrongeſt ſide,
they have nothing more to do, than to acquire
ſuperior force. Now what kind of right can
that be, which vaniſhes with the power of en-
forcing it ? If obedience be only exaᶜted by com-
pulſion, there is no need to make ſuch obedience
a duty, as when we are no longer compelled to
obey, we are no longer obliged to it. It appears, therefore, that the word *right* adds nothing in this caſe to that of force, and, in faᶜt,
is a term of no ſignification.

Be

Be obedient to the higher powers. If by this precept is meant, *subject to a superior force*, the advice is good, though fuperfluous; I will anfwer for it, fuch a rule will never be broken. All power, I own, is derived from God; but every corporeal malady is derived alfo from the fame fource. But are we therefore forbid to call in the phyfician? If a robber fhould ftop me on the highway, am I not only obliged, on compulfion, to give him my purfe, but am I alfo obliged to it in point of confcience, though I might poffibly conceal it from him? This will hardly be averred; and yet the piftol he holds to my breaft, is, in effect, a fuperior force.

On the whole, we muft conclude, then, that mere power doth not conftitute right, and that men are obliged only to pay obedience to lawful authority. Thus we are conftantly recurring to my firft queftion.

CHAP. IV.

On flavery.

AS no man hath any natural authority over the reft of his fpecies, and as power doth not confer right, the bafis of all lawful authority is laid in mutual convention.

If an individual, fays Grotius, can alienate his
liberty, and become the flave of a mafter, why
may not a whole people collectively alienate theirs,
and become fubject to a king ? This propofition,
however, contains fome equivocal terms, which require explanation, but I fhall confine myfelf to
that of *alienate*. Whatever is alienated muft be
difpofed of, either by gift or fale. Now a man
who becomes the flave of another doth not give
himfelf away, but fells himfelf, at leaft for his
fubfiftence ; but why fhould a whole people fell
themfelves ? So far is a king from furnifhing
his fubjects fubfiftence, that they maintain him ;
and, as our friend Rabelais fays, A king doth not
live on a little. Can fubjects be fuppofed to give
away their liberty, on condition that the receiver
fhall take their property along with it ? After
this, I really cannot fee any thing they have left.

It may be faid, a monarch maintains among
his fubjects the public tranquillity. Be it fo ; I
would be glad to know, of what they are gainers, if the wars in which his ambition engages
them, if his infatiable avarice, or the oppreffions
of his minifters, are more deftructive than civil
diffenfions ? Of what are they gainers, if even
this tranquillity be one caufe of their mifery ?
A prifoner may live tranquil enough in his dun-
geon ; but will this be fufficient to make him
contented there ? When the Greeks were fhut
up

up in the cave of the Cyclops, they lived there unmolefted, in expectation of their turn to be devoured.

To fay, that a man can give himfelf away, is to talk unintelligibly and abfurdly; fuch an act muft necefsarily be illegal and void, were it for no other reafon, than that it argues infanity of mind in the agent. To fay the fame thing of a whole people therefore, is to fuppofe a whole nation can be at once out of their fenfes; but were it fo, fuch madnefs could not confer right.

Were it poffible alfo for a man to alienate himfelf, he could not, in the fame manner, difpofe of his children, who, as human beings, are born free; their freedom is their own, and nobody hath any right to difpofe of it but themfelves. Before they arrive at years of difcretion, indeed, their father may, for their fecurity, and in their name, ftipulate the conditions of their prefervation, but he cannot unconditionally and irrevocably difpofe of their perfons, fuch a gift being contrary to the intention of nature, and exceeding the bounds of paternal authority. It is requifite, therefore, in order to render an arbitrary government lawful, that every new generation fhould be at liberty to admit or reject its authority, in which cafe it would be no longer an arbitrary government.

To

To renounce one's natural liberty, is to renounce one's very being as a man; it is to renounce not only the rights, but even the duties of humanity. And what poffible indemnification can be made the man who thus gives up his all? Such a renunciation is incompatible with our very nature; for to deprive us of the liberty of the will, is to take away all morality from our actions. In a word, a convention, which ftipulates on the one part abfolute authority, and on the other implicit obedience, is, in itfelf, futile and contradictory. Is it not evident, that we can lie under no reciprocal obligation whatever to a perfon, of whom we have a right to demand every thing; and doth not this circumftance, againft which he has no equivalent, necefarily infer fuch act of convention to be void? For what claim can my flave have upon me, when he himfelf, and all that belongs to him, are mine? His claims are of courfe my own, and to fay thofe can be fet up againft me, is to talk abfurdly.

Again, Grotius and others have deduced the origin of this pretended right from the fuperiority obtained in war. The conqueror, fay they, having a right to put the vanquifhed to death, the latter may equitably purchafe his life at the expence of his liberty; fuch an agreement being

9   the

the more lawful, as it conduces to the mutual advantage of both parties.

It is clear and certain, however, that this pretended right of the victor over the lives of the vanquished is not, in any shape, the natural result of a state of war. This is plain, were it for no other reason than that the reciprocal relations of mankind, while living together in their primitive independence, were not sufficiently durable, to constitute a state, either of peace or war; so that men cannot be naturally enemies. It is the relation subsisting between things, and not between men, that gives rise to war; which arising thus, not from personal, but real, relations, cannot subsist between man and man, either in a state of nature, in which there is no settled property, or in a state of society, in which every thing is secured by the laws.

The quarrels, encounters and duels of individuals are not sufficient to constitute such a state of war; and, with regard to the particular combats authorised by the institutions of Lewis XI. King of France; they were only some of the abuses of the feudal government, a system truly absurd, as contrary to the principles of natural justice, as of good policy.

War

War is not, therefore, any relation between man and man, but a relation between ftate and ftate, in which individuals are enemies only accidentally, not as men, or even as citizens, but as foldiers; not as members of their particular community, but as its defenders. In fhort, a ftate can have for its enemy nothing but a ftate, not men ; as between things effentially different, there can be no common relation.

This principle is, indeed, conformable to the eftablifhed maxims of all ages, and the conftant practice of every civilized people. Declarations of war are made lefs to give notice to fovereigns, than to their fubjects.

The foreigner, whether a fovereign, an individual, or a people, who plunders, kills, or takes prifoner a fubject, without declaring war againft his prince, is not an enemy, but a robber. Even in a time of war, a juft prince may make himfelf mafter, in an enemy's country, of whatever belongs to the public, but he will refpect the perfons and private properties of individuals; he will refpect thofe rights on which his own are founded. The defign of war being the deftruction of an hoftile ftate, we have a right to kill its defenders, while they are in arms ; but as, in laying down their arms, they ceafe to be enemies,

or

or inftruments of hoftility, they become, in that cafe, mere men, and we have not the leaft right to murder them. It is fometimes poffible effectually to deftroy a ftate, without killing even one of its members; now war cannot confer any right or privilege, which is not neceffary to accomplifh its end and defign. It is true, thefe are not the principles of Grotius, nor are they founded on the authority of the poets; but they are fuch as are deduced from the nature of things, and are founded on reafon.

With regard to the right of conqueft, it has no other foundation than that of force, the law of the ftrongeft. But, if war doth not give the victor a right to maffacre the vanquifhed, this pretended right, which does not exift, cannot be the foundation of a right to enflave them. If we have no right to kill an enemy, unlefs we cannot by force reduce him to flavery, our right to make him a flave never can be founded on our right to kill him. It is, therefore, an iniquitous bargain, to make him purchafe, at the expence of liberty, a life, which we have no right to take away. In eftablifhing thus a right of life and death over others, on that of enflaving them; and, on the other hand, a right of enflaving them on that of life and death, we certainly fall into the abfurdity of reafoning in a circle.

Let

4

Let us suppose, however, that this shocking right of general massacre existed, I still affirm, that a slave, made so by the fortune of war, or a conquered people, so reduced to slavery, lie under no other obligations to their master, than to obey him so long as he hath the power to compel them to it. In accepting of an equivalent for their lives, the victor confers on them no favour; instead of killing them uselessly; he hath only varied the mode of their destruction to his own advantage. So far, therefore, from his having acquired over them any additional authority, the state of war subsists between them as before; their relation to each other is the evident effect of it, and his exertion of the rights of war is a proof, that no treaty of peace hath succeeded. Will it be said, they have made a convention; be it so : This convention is a mere truce, and is so far from putting an end to the state of war, that it necessarily implies its continuation.

Thus, in whatever light we consider this affair, the right of making men slaves is null and void, not only because it is unjust, but because it is absurd and insignificant. The terms *slavery* and *justice* are contradictory and reciprocally exclusive of each other. Hence the following proposal pofal would be equally ridiculous, whether made by one individual to another, or by a private man to a whole people. *I enter into an agreement with you, altogether at your own charge, and folely for my profit, which I will obferve as long as I pleafe, and which you are to obferve alfo, as long as I think proper.*

CHAP. V.

On the neceffity of recurring always to the primitive convention.

ON the fuppofition, that I fhould grant to be true what I have hitherto difproved, the advocate for defpotifm would, however, profit but little. There will be always a great difference between fubjecting a multitude, and governing a fociety. Let individuals, in any number whatever, become feverally and fucceffively fubject to one man, they are all, in that cafe, nothing more than mafter and flaves; they are not a people governed by their chief; they are an Aggregate if you will, but do not form an affociation; there fubfifts among them neither commonwealth nor body politic. Such a fuperior, though he fhould become the mafter of half the world, would be ftill a private perfon, and his intereft, feparate and diftinct from that of his people, would be ftill no more than a

private

private intereſt. When ſuch a perſon dies, alſo
the empire over which he preſided is diſſolved,
and its component parts remain totally uncon-
nected, juſt as an oak falls into a heap of aſhes,
when it is conſumed by the fire.

A people, ſays Grotius, may voluntarily be-
ſtow themſelves on a king: According to Grotius, therefore, a people are a people before
they thus give themſelves up to regal authority.
Even this gift, however, is an act of ſociety, and
preſuppoſes a public deliberation on the matter.
Hence, before we examine into the act, by which
a people make choice of a king, it is proper to
examine into that by which a people became a
people, for, on this, which is neceſſarily prior
to the other, reſts the true foundation of ſociety.

For, if, in fact, there be no prior convention, whence ariſes (unleſs indeed the election
was unanimous) the obligation of the ſmaller
number to ſubmit to the choice of the greater ?
and whence comes it, that an hundred perſons,
for inſtance, who might deſire to have a maſter,
had a right to vote for ten others who might deſire to have none ? The choice by a plurality of
votes is in itſelf an eſtabliſhment of convention,
and ſuppoſes, that unanimity muſt at leaſt for
once have ſubſiſted among them.

CHAP.

CHAP. VI.

On the social pact or covenant.

I Suppose mankind arrived at that term, when the obstacles to their preservation, in a state of nature, prevail over the endeavours of individuals, to maintain themselves in such a state. At such a crisis this primitive state therefore could no longer subsist, and the human race must have perished, if they had not changed their manner of living.

Now as men cannot create new powers, but only compound and direct those which really exist, they have no other means of preservation, than that of forming, by their union, an accumulation of forces, sufficient to oppose the obstacles to their security, and of putting these in action by a first mover, capable of making them act in concert with each other.

This general accumulation of power cannot arise but from the concurrence of many particular forces; but the force and liberty of each individual being the principal instruments of his own preservation, how is he to engage them in the common interest, without hurting his own, and neglecting the obligations he lies under to himself?

himfelf? This difficulty, being applied to my prefent fubject, may be expreffed in the following terms :

" To find that form of affociation which fhall protect and defend, with the whole force of the community, the perfon and property of each individual, and in which each perfon, by uniting himfelf to the reft, fhall neverthelefs be obedient only to himfelf, and remain as fully at liberty as before." Such is the fundamental problem, of which the focial compact gives the folution.

The claufes of this compact are fo precifely determined by the nature of the act, that the leaft reftriction or modification renders them void and of no effect; in fo much, that, although they may perhaps never have been formally promulgated, they are yet univerfally the fame, and are every where tacitly acknowledged and received. When the focial pact, however, is violated, individuals recover their natural liberty, and are re-invefted with their original rights, by lofing that conventional liberty for the fake of which they had renounced them.

Again ; thefe claufes, well underftood, are all reducible to one, *viz.* the total alienation of every individual, with all his rights and privileges,

leges, to the whole community. For, in the firſt place, as every one gives himſelf up entirely and without reſerve, all are in the ſame circumſtances, ſo that no one can be intereſted in making their common connection burthenſome to others.

Beſides, as the alienation is made without reſerve, the union is as perfect as poſſible, nor hath any particular aſſociate any thing to reclaim ; whereas, if they ſhould ſeverally retain any peculiar privileges, there being no common umpire to determine between them and the public, each being his own judge in ſome caſes, would, in time, pretend to be ſo in all, the ſtate of nature would ſtill ſubſiſt, and their aſſociation would neceſſarily become tyrannical or void.

In fine, the individual, by giving himſelf up to all, gives himſelf to none ; and, as he acquires the ſame right over every other perſon in the community, as he gives them over himſelf, he gains an equivalent for what he beſtows, and ſtill a greater power to preſerve what he retains.

If, therefore, we take from the ſocial compact every thing that is not eſſential to it, we ſhall find it reduced to the following terms : " We, the contracting parties, do jointly and ſeverally ſubmit our perſons and abilities, to the ſupreme direction of the general will of all, and, in a collective

collective body, receive each member into that body, as an indivisible part of the whole."

This act of association accordingly converts the several individual contracting parties into one moral collective body, compofed of as many members as there are votes in the affembly, which receives alfo from the fame act its unity and existence. This public perfonage, which is thus formed by the union of all its members, ufed formerly to be denominated a CITY *, and, at prefent,

* The true fenfe of this word is almoft entirely perverted among the moderns; moft people take a town for a city, and an houfe-keeper for a citizen. Such are ignorant, however, that, though houfes may form a town, it is the citizens only that conftitute a city. This fame errour formerly coft the Carthaginians very dear. I do not remember, in the courfe of my reading, to have ever found the title of *Cives* given to the fubjects of a prince, not even formerly to the Macedonians, nor, in our times, to the Englifh, though more nearly bordering on liberty than any other nation. The French are the only people who familiarly take on themfelves the name of *citizens*, becaufe they have no juft idea of its meaning, as may be feen in their dictionaries; for, were it otherwife, indeed, they would be guilty of high treafon in affuming it. This term is with them rather expreffive of a virtue than a privilege. Hence, when Bodin fpoke of the citizens and inhabitants of Geneva,

prefent, takes the name of a *republic*, or *body politic*. It is alfo called, by its feveral members, a *ftate*, when it is paffive; the *fovereign*, when it is active; and fimply a *power*, when it is compared with other bodies of the fame nature. With regard to the affociates themfelves, they take collectively the name of the *people*, and are feparately called *citizens*, as partaking of the fovereign authority, and *fubjects*, as fubjected to the laws of the ftate. Thefe terms, indeed, are frequently confounded, and miftaken one for the other; it is fufficient, however, to be able to diftinguifh them, when they are to be ufed with precifion.

CHAP. VII.

Of the fovereign.

IT is plain from the above formula, that the act of affociation includes a reciprocal engagement between particulars and the public;

neva, he committed a wretched blunder, in miftaking one for the other. Mr. d'Alembert indeed has avoided this miftake in the Encyclopædia, where he has properly diftinguifhed the four orders of people (and even five, reckoning mere ftrangers) that are found in our city, and of which two only compofe the republic: No other French author that I know of hath ever comprehended the meaning of the word *citizen*.

and

and that each individual, in contracting, if I
may fo fay, with himfelf, is laid under a twofold
engagement, *viz.* as a member of the fovereignty toward particular perfons, and as a member
of the ftate toward the fovereign. That
maxim of the civil law, however, is inapplicable
here, which fays, that no one is bound by the
engagements he enters into with himfelf; for
there is a wide difference between entering into
a perfonal obligation with one's felf, and with a
whole, of which one may conftitute a part.

It is farther to be obferved, that the public
determination, which is obligatory on the fubject, with regard to the fovereign, on account
of the twofold relation by which each ftands contracted, is not, for the contrary reafon, obligatory on the fupreme power towards itfelf: and
that it is confequently inconfiftent with the nature of the body politic, that fuch fupreme
power fhould impofe a law, which it cannot
break. For, as the fovereign ftands only in a
fingle relation, it is in the fame cafe as that of an
individual contracting with himfelf; whence it
is plain, that there neither is, nor can be, any
fundamental law obligatory on the whole body
of a people, even the focial compact itfelf not
being fuch. By this, however, it is not meant,
that fuch a body cannot enter into engagements
with others, in matters that do not derogate
from

from this contract; for, with respect to foreign objects, it is a simple and individual person.

But, as the body politic, or the sovereign, derives its very existence from this inviolable contract, it can enter into no lawful engagement, even with any similar body, derogatory from the tenour of this primitive act; such as that of alienating any part of itself, or of submitting itself intirely to a foreign sovereign. To violate the act whereby it exists would be to annihilate itself, and from nothing can arise nothing.

No sooner are a multitude of individuals thus united in a body, than it becomes impossible to act offensively against any of the members, without attacking the whole, and still less to offend the whole body, without injuring the members. Hence both duty and interest equally oblige the two contracting parties to assist each other, and the same persons ought to endeavour to include, within this twofold relation, all the advantages which depend on it.

Now the sovereign, being formed only by the several individuals of which the state is composed, can have no interest contrary to theirs; of course the supreme power stands in no need of any guarantee toward the subjects, because it is

C   impossible,

impoffible, that the body fhould be capable of
hurting all its members; and we fhall fee hereafter, that it can as little tend to injure any of
them in particular.   Hence the fovereign is
neceffarily, and for the fame reafon that it exifts,
always fuch as it ought to be.

. The cafe is different, however, as to the relation in which the fubjects ftand to the fovereign; as, notwithftanding their common intereft, the latter can have no fecurity that the
former will difcharge their engagements, unlefs
means be found to engage their fidelity.

In fact, every individual may, as a man, entertain a particular will, either contradictory or
diffimilar to his general will, as a citizen.   His
private intereft may influence him, in a manner
diametrically oppofite to the common intereft of
the fociety.   Reflecting on his own exiftence as pofitive and naturally independent, he may conceive
what he owes to the common caufe, to be a free
and gratuitous contribution, the want of which
will be lefs hurtful to others, than the difcharge
of it will be burthenfome to himfelf; and, regarding the moral perfon of the ftate as an imaginary being, becaufe it is not a man, he may
be defirous of enjoying all the privileges of a
citizen, without fulfilling his engagement as a
                                                    fubject;

fubject; an injuftice, that, in its progrefs, muft neceffarily be the ruin of the body politic.

To the end, therefore, that the focial compact fhould not prove an empty form, it tacitly includes this engagement, which only can enforce the reft, *viz.* that whofoever refufes to pay obedience to the general will, fhall be liable to be compelled to it by the force of the whole body. And this is in effect nothing more, than that they may be compelled to be free; for fuch is the condition which, in uniting every citizen to the ftate, fecured him from all perfonal dependence; a condition, which forms the whole artifice and play of the political machine: it is this alone that renders all focial engagements juft and equitable which, without it, would be abfurd, tyrannical, and fubject to the moft enormous abufes.

CHAP. VIII.
' *Of civil fociety in general.*

THE tranfition of man from a ftate of nature to a ftate of fociety is productive of a very remarkable change in his being, by fubftituting juftice inftead of inftinct, as the rule of his conduct, and attaching that morality to his actions, of which they were before deftitute. It is in immediate confequence of this change, when

the voice of duty fucceeds to phyfical impulfe
and the law of appetite, that man, who hitherto
regarded only his own gratification, finds himfelf
obliged to act on other principles, and to con-
fult his reafon, before he follows the dictates of
his paffions.   Although, by entering into a ftate
of fociety, he is deprived alfo of many advantages which depend on that of nature, he gains
by it others fo very confiderable, his faculties
exert and expand themfelves, his ideas are en-
larged, his fentiments ennobled, and his whole
foul is elevated to fo great a degree, that, if the
abufes of this new ftate do not degrade him be-
low the former, he ought inceffantly to blefs that
happy moment in which he was refcued from it,
and converted from a ftupid and ignorant animal
into an intelligent and wife Being.

To ftate the balance of what is loft and gained by this change, we fhall reduce it to compa-
rative terms.   By entering into the focial compact, man gives up his natural liberty, or unlimited right to every thing which he is defirous of,
and can attain.   In return for this, he gains focial liberty, and an exclufive property in all
thofe things of which he is poffeffed.   To avoid
any miftake, however, in the nature of thefe
compenfations, it is neceffary to make a juft diftinction between natural liberty, which is limited

2   by

by nothing but the inabilities of the individual, and focial liberty, which is limited by the general will of the community; and alfo, between that poffeffion, which is only effected by force, or follows the right of prior occupancy, and that property, which is founded only on a pofitive title.

To the preceding alfo may be added, as the acquifition of a focial ftate, moral liberty, which only renders a man truly mafter of himfelf: for to be under the direction of appetite alone is to be in a ftate of flavery, while to pay obedience only to thofe laws which we prefcribe to ourfelves, is liberty. But I have faid too much already on this fubject, the philofophical meaning of the word Liberty being, in this place, out of the queftion.

CHAP. IX.

Of real demefnes.

EAch member of the community, in becoming fuch, devotes himfelf to the public from that moment, in fuch a ftate as he then is, with all his power and abilities, of which abilities his poffeffions make a part. Not that in confequence of this act the poffeffion changes its nature, by changing hands, and becomes actual

C 3 property

property in thofe of the fovereignty; but as the power of the community is incomparably greater than that of an individual, the public poffeffion is in fact more fixed and irrevocable, without being more lawful, at leaft with regard to foreigners. For every ftate is, with refpect to its members, mafter of all their poffeffions, by virtue of the focial compact, which, in a ftate, ferves as the bafis of all other rights; but, with regard to other powers or ftates, it is mafter of them only, by the right of prior occupancy, which it derives from individuals.

The right of prior occupancy, although more real than that of the ftrongeft, becomes not an equitable right, till after the eftablifhment of property. Every man hath naturally a right to every thing which is neceffary for his fubfiftence; but the pofitive act by which he is made the proprietor of a certain poffeffion excludes him from the property of any other. His portion being affigned him, he ought to confine himfelf to that, and hath no longer any right to a community of poffeffion. Hence it is that the right of prior occupancy, though but of little force in a ftate of nature, is fo refpectable in that of fociety. The point to which we are chiefly directed in the confideration of this right, is rather

ther what belongs to another, than what does not belong to us.

To define the right of prior occupancy in general terms, it is founded on the following conditions. It is requisite, in the first place, that the lands in question should be unoccupied; secondly, that no greater quantity of it should be occupied than is necessary for the subsistence of the occupiers; and, in the third place, that possession should be taken of it, not by a vain ceremony, but by actual cultivation, the only mark of property, which, in defect of juridical titles, should be at all respected.

To allow the first occupier a right to as much territory as he may cultivate, and is necessary to his subsistence, is certainly carrying the matter as far as is reasonable. Otherwise we know not how to set bounds to this right. Is it sufficient for a man to set foot on an uninhabited territory, to pretend immediately an exclusive right to it? Is it sufficient for him to have power enough at one time to drive others from the spot, to deprive them for ever afterwards of the right of returning to it? How can a man, or even a whole people, possess themselves of an immense territory, and exclude from it the rest of mankind, without

C 4   being

being guilty of an illegal ufurpation; fince, by fo doing, they deprive the reft of mankind of an habitation, and thofe means of fubfiftence, which nature hath given in common to them all? When Nunez Balbao ftood on the fea-fhore, and, in the name of the crown of Caftile, took poffef-fion of the Pacific Ocean, and of all South-America, was this fufficient to difpoffefs all the inhabitants of that vaft country, and exclude all the other fovereigns in the world? On fuch a fuppofition, the like idle ceremonies might have been ridiculoufly multiplied, and his Catholic Majefty would have had no more to do, than to have taken poffeffion in his clofet of all the coun-tries in the world, and to have afterwards only deduced from his empire fuch as were before poffeffed by other princes.

It is eafy to conceive, how the united and contiguous eftates of individuals become the ter-ritory of the public, and in what manner the right of fovereignty, extending itfelf from the fubjects to the lands they occupy, becomes at once both real and perfonal; a circumftance which lays the poffeffors under a ftate of the greateft dependence, and makes even their own abilities a fecurity for their fidelity. This is an

advantage

advantage which does not appear to have been duly attended to, by fovereigns among the ancients, who, by ftiling themfelves only kings of the Perfians, the Scythians, the Macedonians, feemed to look on themfelves only as chief of men, rather than as mafters of a country. Modern princes more artfully ftile themfelves the kings of England, France, Spain, &c. and thus, by claiming the territory itfelf, are fecure of the inhabitants.

What is very fingular in this alienation is, that the community, in accepting the poffeffions of individuals, is fo far from defpoiling them thereof, that, on the contrary, it only confirms them in fuch poffeffions, by converting an ufurpation into an actual right, and a bare poffeffion into a real property. The poffeffors alfo being confidered as the depofitaries of the public wealth, while their rights are refpected by all the members of the ftate, and maintained by all its force againft any foreign power, they acquire, if I may fo fay, by a ceffion advantageous to the public, and ftill more fo to themfelves, every thing they ceded by it: a paradox which is eafily explained by the diftinction to be made between the rights which the fovereign and the

C 5   proprietor

proprietor have in the fame fund, as will be feen hereafter.

It may alfo happen, that men may form them-felves into a fociety, before they have any pof-feffions ; and that, acquiring a territory fufficient for all, they may poffefs it in common, or di-vide it among them, either equally, or in fuch different proportions as may be determined by the fovereign. Now, in whatfoever manner fuch acquifition may be made, the right which each individual has to his own eftate, muft be al-ways fubordinate to the right which the com-munity hath over the poffeffions of all ; for, without this, there would be nothing binding in the focial tie, nor any real force in the exer-cife of the fupreme power.

I fhall end this book, with a remark, that ought to ferve as the bafis of the whole focial fyftem : and this is, that, inftead of annihilating the natural equality among mankind, the funda-mental compact fubftitutes, on the contrary, a moral and legal equality, to make up for that natural and phyfical difference which prevails among individuals, who, though unequal in per-

fonal

fonal ftrength and mental abilities, become thus all equal by convention and right *.

* This equality, indeed, is under fome govern-ments merely apparent and delufive, ferving only to keep the poor ftill in mifery, and favour the oppref-fion of the rich. And, in fact, the laws are always ufeful to perfons of fortune, and hurtful to thofe who are deftitute: whence it follows, that a ftate of fo-ciety is advantageous to mankind in general, only when they all poffefs fomething, and none of them have any thing too much.

The END of the FIRST BOOK.

C 6   BOOK

BOOK II.

CHAP. I.

That the sovereignty is unalienable.

THE firſt and moſt important conſequence to be drawn from the principles already eſtabliſhed, is, that the general *will* only can direct the forces of the ſtate agreeable to the end of its original inſtitution, which is the common good; for, though the oppoſition of private intereſts might make the eſtabliſhment of ſocieties neceſſary, it muſt have been through the coalition of thoſe intereſts, that ſuch eſtabliſhment became poſſible. The bonds of ſociety muſt have been formed out of ſomething common to thoſe ſeveral intereſts, for, if there had been no point to which they could have been reconciled, no ſociety could poſſibly have ſubſiſted. Now it is only on theſe points that the government of ſociety ſhould be founded.

I ſay, therefore, that the ſovereignty, being only the exertion of the general will, cannot be alienated, and that the ſovereign, which is only a collective being, cannot be repreſented but by itſelf:

itfelf: the power of a people may be tranfmitted
or delegated, but not their will.

It may not be abfolutely impoffible, that the
will of an individual fhould agree, in fome particular point, with the general will of a whole
people ; it is, however, impoffible, that fuch
agreement fhould be conftant and durable, for
the will of particulars always tends to make diftinctions of preference, and the general will to
a perfect equality. It is further ftill more impoffible, fuppofing fuch agreement might always
fubfift, to have any fecurity that it would do fo,
as it could never be the effect of art, but of
chance. The fovereign may fay, My will is now
agreeable to the will of fuch an individual, or at
leaft to what he pretends to be his will ; but it
cannot pretend to fay, I agree to whatever may
be the will of fuch individual to-morrow ; as it
is abfurd for the will to lay itfelf under any reftraint regarding the future, and as it is impoffible for the will to confent to any thing contrary
to the intereft of the being whofe will it is.
Should a people therefore enter into the engagement of fimply promifing obedience, they would
lofe their quality, as a people, and be virtually
diffolved by that very act. The moment there
exifts a mafter, there can be no longer a fovereign, the body politic being thereby deftroyed.
I would

I would not be underftood to mean, that the orders of a chief may not pafs for the dictates of the general will, when the fovereign, though at liberty to contradict, does not oppofe it. In fuch a cafe, it is to be prefumed, from the univerfal filence of the people, that they give their confent. This will be farther explained in the end.

CHAP. II.

That the fovereignty is indivifible.

FOR the fame reafon that the fovereignty is unalienable, it is alfo indivifible; for the will is general *, or it is not; it is that of the body of the people, or only that of a part. In the firft cafe, this will, when declared, is an act of fovereignty, and becomes a law: in the fecond, it is only a particular will, or an act of the magiftracy, and is at moft a decree.

But our politicians, incapable of dividing the fovereignty in its firft principles, divide it in its

* In order that this will fhould be general, it is not always neceffary it fhould be unanimous : it is neceffary, however, that every individual fhould be permitted to vote; every formal exclufion infringing the generality.

object;

object; they diftinguifh it into power and will; into a legiflative and executive power; into the prerogatives of taxation, of executing juftice, and of making war; into departments of do-meftic and foreign adminiftration. Sometimes they blend all thefe confufedly together, and, at others, confider them as diftinct and feparate, making out the fovereign to be a fantaftic com-pound, juft as if they fhould compofe a man out of feveral bodies, of which one fhould have on-ly eyes, another arms, a third feet, and nothing more. It is faid of the jugglers in Japan, that they will take a child, and cut it into pieces in the prefence of the fpectators, then, throwing up its difmembered limbs one after another into the air, they are united, and the child defcends alive, and well as before. The legerdemain of our modern politicians greatly refembles this trick of the Japonefe; for they, after having difmem-bered the body politic with equal dexterity, bring all its parts together by *hocus pocus* again, and reprefent it the fame as before.

This error arifes from their not having form-ed precife ideas of the fovereign authority, and from their miftaking the fimple emanations of this authority, for parts of its effence. Thus, for inftance, the acts of declaring war and ma-king peace are ufually regarded as acts of fovereignty,

reignty, which they are not; for neither of these acts are laws, but confist only of the application of the law. Each is a particular act, determinate only of the meaning of the law in such case, as will be seen more clearly, when the idea attached to the word *law* shall be precisely settled.

By tracing, in like manner, their other divisions, we shall find, that we are constantly mistaken, whenever we think the sovereignty divided; and that the prerogatives, which are supposed to be parts of the sovereignty, are all subordinate to it, and always suppose the predetermination of a superior will, which those prerogatives only serve to put in execution.

It is impossible to say, in how much obscurity this want of precision hath involved the reasonings of authors, on the subject of political law, when they came to examine into the respective rights of kings and people, on the principles they had established. By turning to the third and fourth chapters of the first book of Grotius, the reader may see, how that learned author and his translator, Barbeyrac, bewildered and entangled themselves in their own sophisms, through fear of saying too much or too little for their purpose, and of making those interests clash, which

which it was their bufinefs to reconcile. Grotius, being diffatisfied with his own countrymen, a refugee in France, and willing to pay his court to Lewis XIII. to whom his book is dedicated, fpared no art nor pains to ftrip the people of their privileges, and to inveft kings with prerogative. Barbeyrac alfo wrote with a fimilar view, dedicating his tranflation to George I. of England. But, unluckily, the expulfion of James II. which he calls an abdication, obliged him to be much on the referve, to turn and wind about, as he faw occafion, in order not to make William III. an ufurper. Had thefe two writers adopted true principles, all thefe difficulties would have vanifhed, and they would have written confiftently ; in fuch a cafe, however, they could only, in fober fadnefs, have told the truth, and would have paid their court only to the people. Now, to tell the truth, is not the way to make a fortune ; nor are ambaffadors appointed, or places and penfions given away by the populace.

CHAP.

CHAP. III.

Whether the general Will can be in the wrong.

IT follows, from what has been said, that the general Will is always in the right, and constantly tends to the public good ; it does not follow, however, that the deliberations of the people will always be attended with the same rectitude.   We are ever defirous of our own good, but we do not always diftinguifh in what it confifts.   A whole people never can be corrupted, but they may be often miftaken, and it is in fuch a cafe only that they appear to feek their own difadvantage.

There is often a confiderable difference between the will of all the members and the general will of the whole body ; the latter regards only the common intereft, the other refpects the private intereft of individuals, and is the aggregated fum of their particular wills ; but, if we take from this fum thofe contradictory wills that mutually deftroy each other *, the fum of the remaining differences is the general will.

If

---

* *Each intereft,* fays the Marquis d'A. *has different principles.   A coalition between two particular interefts may be formed, out of oppofition to that of a third.* He
                                        might

If a people, sufficiently informed of the nature of the subject under their consideration, should deliberate, without having any communication with each other, the general will would always result from the greater number of their little differences, and their deliberation would be such as it ought to be. But when they enter into cabals, and form partial associations, at the expence of the general one, the will of each of these associations becomes general, with regard to the particular members of each, and, in itself, particular, with regard to the state. In such a case, therefore, it may be said, there is no longer as many voters as individuals, but only as many voices as there are associations. The differences then become less numerous, and give a less general result. Again, should one of these partial associations be so great, as to influence all the rest, the result would no longer be the sum of many little differences, but that of one great one; in which case, a general will would no longer subsist.

might have added, that a coalition of all is formed out of opposition to the interest of each. Were there no different and clashing interests, that of the whole would be hardly distinguishable, as it would meet with no obstacle. All things would go regularly on of their own accord, and civil policy would cease to be an art.

It

It is requifite, therefore, in order that each re-
folution may be dictated by the general will,
that no fuch partial focieties fhould be formed in
a ftate, and that each citizen fhould think for
himfelf *.   Such was the fublime inftitution of
the great Lycurgus.   But, if fuch partial focieties muft and will exift, it is then expedient
to multiply their number, and prevent their inequality, as was done by Solon, Numa, and
Servius.   Thefe are the only falutary precautions
that can be taken, in order that the general will
may be properly informed, and the people not
be miftaken as to their true intereft.

C H A P.   IV.

Of the limits of the fovereign power.

IF the ftate, or the city, be a mere moral
perfon, whofe life depends on the union of
its members, and, if the moft important of its
concerns be that of its own prefervation, it

* Vera cofa é, fays Machiavel, che alcuni divifi-
oni nuocono alle republiche, e alcune giovano : quelle
nuocono che fono dalle fette e da partigiani accom-
pagnate : quelle giovano che fenza fette, fenza partigiani fi mantengono.   Non potendo adunque prove-
dere un fondatore d'una republica che non fiano nimi-
cizie in quella, hà da proveder almeno che non vifia-
no fette.   Hift. Fiorent. l. vii.

fhould

should certainly be possessed of an universal compulsive force,. to move and dispose each part in such a manner as is most conducive to the good of all. As nature hath given every man an absolute power over his limbs, to move and direct them at pleasure, so the social compact gives to the body politic an absolute power over all its members, and it is this power which, directed by the general will, bears the name, as I have already observed, of the sovereignty.

But, besides this public person, we are to consider farther the private persons of which it is composed, and whose life and liberty are naturally independent of it. We come now, therefore, to make a proper distinction between the respective privileges of the citizens and the sovereign *, as well as between the obligations the former lie under as subjects, and the natural rights they claim as men.

It is agreed, that what an individual alienates of his power, his possession, or his liberty, by the social compact, is only such parts of them whose use is of importance to the community;

* Be not in haste, attentive reader, to accuse me here of contradiction. I cannot avoid the seeming contradiction in terms, from the native poverty of the language. But have a little patience.

but

but it muſt be confeſſed alſo, that the ſovereign is the only proper judge of this importance.

A citizen is bound to perform all the ſervices he can poſſibly be of to a ſtate, whenever the ſovereign demands them ; but the ſovereign, on his part, cannot require any thing of the ſubject that is uſeleſs to the community ; he cannot even be deſirous of ſo doing ; for, under the laws of reaſon, nothing can be produced without a cauſe, any more than under the law of nature.

The engagements, in which we are bound to the body of ſociety, are obligatory, only becauſe they are mutual ; and their nature is ſuch that we cannot, in diſcharging them, labour for the good of others, without, at the ſame time, labouring for that of ourſelves. Wherefore, indeed, is it, that the general will is always in the right, and that all conſtantly deſire the good of each, unleſs it be, becauſe there is no one that does not appropriate the term *each* to himſelf, and who does not think of his own intereſt, in voting for that of all ? This ſerves to prove alſo, that an equality of privilege, and the notion of juſtice it produces, are derived from that preference which each naturally gives himſelf, and of courſe from the very nature of man ; that the

I   general

general will, in order to be truly fuch, ought
to be fo in its effect, as well as in its effence ;
that it ought to flow from all, in order to be applicable to all ; and that it muft lofe its natural
rectitude, when it tends to any individual and
determinate object ; becaufe judging, in fuch a
cafe, of what is foreign to ourfelves, we have
no real principle of equity for our guide.

In fact, no fooner do we come to treat of a
particular fact or privilege, on a point which
has not been fettled by a general and prior convention, than the affair becomes litigious. It is
a procefs, in which the particulars interefted are
one party, and the public the other ; but in
which I fee no law to decide, nor judge to determine. It would be abfurd, therefore, in fuch
a cafe, to think of referring it to any exprefs decifion of the general will, which could be no
other than the decifion of one of the very parties ; and therefore muft be, with regard to the
other, foreign and partial, leaning to injuftice,
and fubject to error. In the fame manner, alfo,
that a partial and particular will cannot reprefent the general will, fo the latter, in its turn,
changes its nature, when employed on a particular object, and cannot, in its general capacity,
pronounce concerning any particular man or fact.
Thus, when the people of Athens, for inftance,
took

took upon them to appoint or cafhier their chiefs, to decree honours to one, and inflict pains and penalties on another, and thus, by numerous decrees, exercifed indifcriminately all the acts of government, they had then, properly fpeaking, no general will at all: the Athenian people, in this cafe, did not act in the capacity of fovereign, but in that of magiftrate. This may appear contradictory to the common notions of things, but I muft be allowed time to explain mine.

We may learn hence, that the general will confifts lefs in the number of votes, than in the common intereft that unites them ; for, in this inftitution, every one fubjects himfelf necefarily to thofe conditions which he impofes on others : hence the admirable conformity between intereft and juftice, which ftamps on public declarations that characteriftic of equity, which we fee vanifh in the difcuffion of particular fubjects, for want of that common intereft which unites and . makes the criterion of the judge the fame with that of the party.

In what manner foever we recur to the firft principle, we always arrive at the fame conclufion, *viz.* that the focial compact eftablifhes fuch an equality among the citizens, that all lay
themfelves

themſelves under the ſame obligations, and ought all to enjoy the ſame privileges. Thus, from the very nature of this compact, every act of ſovereignty, that is to ſay, every authentic act of the general will, is equally obligatory on, or favourable to, all the citizens, without diſtinction ; in ſo much that the ſovereign knows only the whole body of the nation, but diſtinguiſhes none of the individuals who compoſe it. What then is properly an act of ſovereignty ? It is not an agreement made between a ſuperior and an inferior, but a convention between a whole body with each of its members, which convention is a lawful one, becauſe founded on the ſocial contract ; it is equitable, becauſe it is common to all ; it is uſeful, becauſe it can have no other object than the general good ; and it is ſolid and durable, becauſe ſecured by the public ſtrength and the ſupreme power.

When the ſubmiſſion of ſubjects is owing only to ſuch conventions, they pay in fact obedience to none but their own will, and to aſk how far the reſpective privileges of the ſovereign and citizens extend, is to aſk merely how far the latter may enter into engagements with themſelves, *viz*, each individual with all collectively, and all collectively with each individual.

Hence

Hence we fee, that the fovereign power, abfolute, inviolable, and facred as it is, neither
does nor can furpafs the bounds of fuch general
conventions, and that every man hath a right to
difpofe, as he pleafes, of that liberty and property which the terms of fuch conventions have
left to his own difpofal ; fo that the fovereign
hath not any right to lay a greater burthen on
one fubject than on another, becaufe, in fuch a
cafe, it becomes a particular affair, in which the
fovereign hath no power to act.

These diftinctions being once admitted, it is
fo far from being true, that there is any real renunciation on the part of individuals, when
they enter into the focial compact, that their fituation becomes, by means of that very compact,
much better than before ; as, inftead of making
any alienation, they only make an advantageous
exchange of an uncertain and precarious mode
of fubfiftence, for a more fettled and determinate one ; they exchange their natural independence, for focial liberty, the power of injuring others for that of fecuring themfelves from
injury ; and their own natural ftrength, which
might be overcome by that of others, for a civil
power which the focial union renders invincible.
Their very lives, which they have by thefe means
de--

devoted to the state, are continually protected ; and even when they are obliged to expose themselves to death, in its defence, what do they more than render back to society what they have before received of it ? What do they more, in risquing their lives for their country, than they would have been obliged to do more frequently, and with much greater danger in a state of nature ; when, subject to inevitable outrages, they would have been obliged to defend their means of subsistance at the hazard of their lives ? That every one lies under the obligation of fighting in defence of his country, is true ; but then he is relieved by the laws from the necessity of fighting to defend himself. And are not men gainers, on the whole, by running part of those risks, for their common security, which they must severally run for themselves, were they deprived of that security ?

CHAP. V.

On capital punishments.

IT hath been asked, how individuals, having no right to dispose of their own lives, can transmit that right to the sovereign ? The difficulty of resolving this question, arises only from

its

its being badly expreſſed. Every man hath an un-
doubted right to hazard his life for its preſervation.
Was a man ever charged with ſuicide, for throwing himſelf from the top of an houſe in flames, in
order to avoid being burnt? Was it ever im-
puted as a crime to a man, who might be caſt
away at ſea, that he knew the danger of the
voyage when he embarked?

The end of the ſocial compact, is the preſervation of the contracting parties. Such,
therefore, as would reap the benefit of the end,
muſt aſſent to the means, which are inſeparable
from ſome dangers and loſſes. He that would preſerve his life at the expence of others, ought
to riſk it for their ſafety when it is neceſſary.
Now, the citizen is no longer a judge of the danger to which the law requires him to be expoſed:
but when the prince declares that the good of
the ſtate requires his life, he ought to reſign it;
ſince it is only on thoſe conditions he hath hitherto lived in ſecurity, and his life is not
ſolely the gift of nature, but a conditional gift
of the ſtate.

The puniſhment of death inflicted on malefactors may be conſidered alſo in the ſame point
of view: it is to prevent our falling by the
hands

hands of an affaffin, that we confent to die, on becoming fuch ourfelves. We are fo far from giving away our lives, by this treaty, that we enter into it only for our prefervation : as 't is not to be prefumed that any one of the contracting parties formed therein a premeditated defign to get himfelf hanged.

Add to this, that every malefactor, by breaking the laws of his country, becomes a rebel and traitor; ceafing, from that time, to be a member of the community, and even declaring war againft it. In this cafe, the prefervation of the ftate is incompatible with his; one of the two muft perifh: and thus when a criminal is executed, he doth not fuffer in the quality of a citizen, but in that of an enemy. His trial and fentence are the evidence and declaration of his having broken the focial compact; and that, of confequence, he is no longer a member of the ftate. Now, as he had profeffed himfelf fuch, at leaft by his refidence, it is right that he fhould be feparated from the ftate, either by banifhment as a violator of the focial compact, or by death as a public enemy; for fuch an enemy is not a moral perfonage, he is a mere man, and it is in this cafe only that the right of war takes place of killing an enemy.

But,

But, it may be said, the condemnation of a criminal is a particular act. It is so, and for that reason it does not belong to the sovereign : it is an act, for doing which the supreme power may confer the authority, though it cannot ex-ercise such authority itself. My ideas on this 'subject are confistent, though I cannot explain them all at once.

It is to be observed, however, that the fre-quency of executions is always a sign of the weakness or indolence of government. There is no malefactor who might not be made good for something : Nor ought any person to be put to death, even by way of example, unless such as could not be preserved without endangering the community.

With regard to the prerogative of granting pardons to criminals, condemned by the laws of their country, and sentenced by the judges, it belongs only to that power which is superior both to the judges and the laws, viz. the sove-reign authority. Not that it is very clear that even the supreme power is vested with such a right, or that the circumstances in which it might be exerted are frequent or determinate. In a well-governed state there are but few execu-tions;

tions; not becaufe there are many pardoned, but becaufe there are few criminals : Whereas when a ftate is on the decline, the multiplicity of crimes occafions their impunity. Under the Roman republic, neither the Senate nor the Con- fuls ever attempted to grant pardons ; even the people never did this, although they fometimes recalled their own fentence. The frequency of pardons indicates that in a fhort time crimes will not ftand in need of them, and every one may fee the confequence of fuch conduct. But my reluctant heart reftrains my pen ; let us leave the difcuffion of thefe queftions to the juft man who hath never been criminal, and who never ftood in need of pardon.

CHAP. VI.

On the law.

HAVING given exiftence and life to the body politic, by a focial compact, we come now to give it action and will, by a legifla- ture. For the primitive act, by which fuch body is formed, determines nothing as yet with refpect to the means of its prefervation.

Whatever is right and conformable to order, is fuch from the nature of things, independent

of

of all human conventions. All juſtice comes from God, who is the fountain of it ; but could we receive it immediately from ſo ſublime a ſource, we ſhould ſtand in no need of government or laws. There is indeed an univerſal juſtice ſpring-ing from reaſon alone ; but, in order to admit this to take place among mankind, it ſhould be reciprocal. To conſider things as they appear, we find the maxims of juſtice among mankind, to be vain and fruitleſs, for want of a natural ſupport; they tend only to the advantage of the wicked, and the diſadvantage of the juſt, while the latter obſerves them in his behaviour to others, but no body regards them in their conduct to him. Laws and conventions, therefore, are neceſſary in order to unite duties with privileges, and confine juſtice to its proper objects. In a ſtate of nature, where every thing is common, I owe nothing to thoſe I have promiſed nothing; I acknowlege nothing to be the property of an-other, but what is uſeleſs to myſelf. In a ſtate of ſociety the caſe is different, where the rights of each are fixed by law.

We come at length, therefore, to conſider what is law. So long as we content ourſelves with the metaphyſical idea annexed to this term, we muſt talk unintelligibly ; and though we

ſhould

fhould come to a definition of natural law, we fhould not know thence any thing more of political law. I have already faid there can be no general will relative to a particular object. In fact every particular object muft be within or without the ftate. If without, a will that is foreign, cannot with regard to it be general; and if the object be within the ftate, it muft make a part of it: in which cafe there arifes between the whole and the part, a relation that conftitutes two feparate beings, one of which is the part, and the whole wanting fuch part, is the other. But the whole wanting fuch part, is not the whole, and fo long as that relation fubfifts, there is no whole, but only two unequal parts: whence it follows that the will of the one is no longer general with regard to that of the other.

But when a whole people decree concerning a whole people, they confider only their whole body; and, if it then forms any relation, it muft be between the entire object confidered in one point of view, and the entire object confidered in another point of view, without any divifion of the whole. In this cafe, the matter of the decree is general as the will that decrees. Such is the act which I call a law.

D 5   When

When I fay that the object of the laws is always general, I mean that the law confiders the
fubjects in a collective body, and their actions
abitractedly, but never concerns itfelf with individual perfons, nor particular actions. Thus
the law may decree certain privileges, but it
cannot beftow them on particular perfons : the
law may conftitute feveral claffes of citizens,
and affign even the qualities which may entitle
them to rank in thefe claffes ; but it cannot nominate fuch or fuch perfons to be admitted
therein: It may eftablifh a legal government,
and appoint an hereditary fucceffion, but it cannot make choice of a king, nor appoint the royal
family ; in a word, every function that relates to
an individual object, doth not belong to the legiflative power.

   Taking things in this light, it is immediately
feen how abfurd it is to afk in whofe power it is
to make laws ? as they are acts of the general
will ; or whether the prince be above the laws ?
as he is but a member of the ftate.   Hence alfo,
it is plain, the law cannot be unjuft, as nothing
can be unjuft to itfelf ; as alfo what it is to be
free, and at the fame time fubject to the laws,
as the laws are only the records of our own
will.

                                                    It

It is hence farther evident, the law re-uniting the univerfality of the will to that of its object that whatever an individual, of what rank fo-ever, may decree of his own head, cannot be a law : indeed, whatever the fupreme power itfelf may ordain concerning a particular object is not a law, but a fimple decree ; it is not an act of the fovereignty, but of the magiftracy.

I call every ftate, therefore, which is govern-ed by laws, a Republic, whatever be the form of its adminiftration ; for in fuch a cafe only, it is the public intereft that governs, and what-ever is public is fomething. Thus every lawful government is republican *. I fhall explain hereafter what I mean by a government.

The laws are, ftrictly fpeaking, only the con-ditions of civil fociety. The people who fub-

---

* I do not here mean, by the term republican, either an ariftocracy or democracy ; but in general every go-vernment influenced by the general will of the people, which is the law. To make a government legal, it is not neceffary that it fhould be confounded with the fovereign, but that it fhould be the minifter : fo that in this fenfe even a monarchy is a republic. This will be more fully explained in the fubfequent book.

mit to them fhould therefore be the authors of
them ; as it certainly belongs to the affociating
parties, to fettle the conditions on which they
agree to form a fociety. But how are they to
be fettled ? is it to be done by common confent
or by a fudden infpiration ? hath the body politic an organ by which to make known its will ?
who fhall furnifh it with the neceffary prefcience
to form its determinations, and to publifh them
before-hand, or how fhall it divulge them in the
time of need ? how fhall an ignorant multitude,
who often know not what they chufe, becaufe
they feldom know what is for their good, execute an enterprize fo great and fo difficult as
that of a fyftem of legiflature ? A people muft
neceffarily be defirous of their own good, but
they do not always fee in what it confifts. The
general will is always in the right, but the
judgment by which it is directed is not always
fufficiently informed. It is neceffary it fhould
fee objects fuch as they are, and fometimes fuch
as they ought to appear ; it fhould be directed
to the falutary end it would purfue, fhould be
fecured from the feduction of private interefts,
fhould have an infight into the circumftances
of time and place ; and fhould be enabled to
fet the prefent and perceptible advantages of
things, againft the diftant and concealed evil

that

.that may attend them. Individuals often fee
the good which they reject ; the public is de-.
firous of that which it is incapable to fee. Both
ftand equally . in need of a guide : the former
fhould be compelled to conform their defires to
reafon, and the latter fhould be inftructed in the
difcovery of what it defires. It is thus from the
proper information of the public, that there refults an union of the underftanding and the will
in the body of fociety, and thence the exact
concurrence of its parts, and in the end the
greateft force of the whole. Hence arifes the
neceffity of a legiflator.

C H A P. VII.

Of the genius and character of a legiflator.

·TO inveftigate thofe conditions of fociety
which may beft anfwer the purpofes of
nations, would require the abilities of fome fuperior intelligence, who fhould be witnefs to all
the paffions of men, but be fubject itfelf to
none ; who fhould have no connection with
human nature, but fhould have a perfect knowlege of it ; a being, in fhort, whofe happinefs fhould be independent of us, and who
would

would neverthelefs employ itfelf about ours *.
. It is the province of Gods indeed to make laws
for men.

The fame argument which Caligula made ufe
of, in point of fact, Plato himfelf employs, in
point of right, when he goes about to define the civil or royal perfonage, in treating of
a king. But if it be certain that a great prince
is a perfonage rarely to be met with, what is
that of a great legiflator ? The former hath nothing more to do than to follow the model defigned by the latter. The one is the mechanical
genius who invents the machine, the other only
the workman who puts it into execution. In
the commencement of focieties, fays Montefquieu, it is the principal perfons in republics
which form their inftitution ; and afterwards it
is the inftitution which forms the chiefs of republics.

He who fhould undertake to form a body politic, ought to perceive himfelf capable of work-
ing a total change in human nature ; of tranf-
forming every individual, of himfelf a folitary

* Nations become famous only as their legiflature
declines. The inftitution of Lycurgus made the
Spartans happy for ages before they were famous in
Greece.

and

and independent being, into a part of a greater whole, from which such individual is to receive in one sense his life and existence ; he must be capable of altering the constitution of the man, in order to strengthen it ; and to substitute a partial and moral existence in the room of that physical and independent existence which we receive from the hands of Nature. In a word, he must be able to deprive man of his natural abilities, in order to invest him with foreign powers which he cannot make use of without the assistance of others. The more such natural force is annihilated and extinct, the greater and more durable are those which are acquired, and the more perfect and solid is the social institution. So that if each citizen be nothing, and can effect nothing but by the existence and assistance of all the rest, and that the force acquired by the whole body be equal, or superior, to the sum of the natural forces of all its individuals, the legislature may be said to have reached the highest pitch of perfection it is capable to attain.

The legislator is in every respect a most extraordinary person in a state. If he be undoubtedly so, on account of his genius, he is not less so from his function. Yet this is not that of the

ma-

magiftrate or the fovereign. : That function, which conftitutes the republic, doth not enter into its conftitution. It is, on the contrary, a particular and fuperior employment that hath nothing in common with human government : for if he who hath the command over the citizens, fhould not be entrufted with the command over the laws, he who hath the power over the laws, ought as little to have the power over the ci- tizens: for were it otherwife, his laws, being made inftrumental to his paffions, would often ferve to perpetuate his injuftice, and he could never pre- vent particular views from altering his fyftem.

When Lycurgus gave laws to his country, he began by abdicating the throne. It was the cuftom of moft of the Grecian cities to entruft their eftablifhment with ftrangers; a cuftom that hath been often imitated by the modern republics of Italy : that of Geneva did the fame, and found its account in it *. In the moft

* Thofe who confider Calvin only as a theologift, know but little of his comprehenfive genius. The digeft of our laws, in which he had a confider- able fhare, do him as much honour as his religious fyftem; and what revolution foever time may effect in our public worfhip, the memory of this great man will continue to be revered fo long as patriotifm and a fenfe of liberty furvive among us.

flourifh-

flourishing age of Rome, that city suffered under flagitious acts of tyranny, and beheld itself
on the brink of ruin, for having entrusted the
sovereign power and the legiflative authority in
the fame hands.

Even the decemviri themselves, however, never affumed the right of paffing any law merely
on their own authority. *Nothing that we pro-
pofe*, faid they to the people, *can pafs into a law
without your confent. Be yourfelves, ye Romans,
the authors of thofe laws on which your happinefs
depends.*

The legiflator, therefore, who digefts the
laws, fhould have no right to make them pafs
for fuch ; nor indeed can the people, though
inclined to do it, deprive themfelves of that in-
communicable right : becaufe, according to the
fundamental compact, it is the general will only
that is obligatory on individuals, and it is impoffible to be affured that any particular will is
conformable to the general, till it be fubmitted
to on the free fuffrage of the people. I have faid
this before, but perhaps have not unneceffarily
repeated it.

Thus

Thus in the bufinefs of a legiflature, we find two things apparently incompatible ; a defign fuperior to human abilities, carried into execution by an authority which is nothing.

Another difficulty which merits attention is, that wife men, in talking their own language to the vulgar, fpeak unintelligibly. And yet there are many kinds of ideas which it is impoffible to convey in the language of the people. Views too general, and objects too diftant, are equally beyond their comprehenfion ; the individual, relifhing no other plan of government than that which is conducive to his private intereft, is with difficulty brought to fee thofe advantages which are to be deduced from the continual checks he may receive from falutary laws. In order to give a newly-formed people a tafte for the found maxims of policy, and induce them to follow the fundamental rules of fociety, it is neceffary that the effect fhould in a manner become the caufe ; that the fpirit of union which fhould be the effect of focial inftitutions fhould prefide to form that inftitution itfelf, and that men fhould be fuch before the laws are made as the laws are defigned to make them. For this reafon therefore, the legiflator being capable of employing neither force nor argument,

he

he is of neceffity obliged to recur to an authority of an higher order, which may compel
without violence, and perfuade without con-
viction. Hence it is that the founders of nations have been obliged, in all ages, to
recur to the intervention of celeftial powers,
and have honoured their gods with their own
wifdom, in order that the people, by fubmitting themfelves to the laws of the ftate in the
fame manner as to thofe of nature, and acknow-
leging the fame power in the formation of the
city as in the formation of man, might bend
more freely, and bear more tractably the yoke
of obedience and public felicity.

Now the determinations of that fublime reafon, which foars above the comprehenfion of
vulgar minds, are thofe which the legiflator puts
into the mouths of his immortal perfonages,
in order to influence thofe by a divine authoiity,
which could not be led by maxims of human
prudence. It does not belong to every man,
however, to make the gods his oracles, nor
even to be believed when he pretends to be their
interpreter. The comprehenfive genius of the
legiflator, is the miracle that proves the truth of
his miffion. Any man may engrave tables of
ftone, hire an oracle, pretend to a fecret com-
munica-

munication with some deity, teach a bird to whisper in his ear, or hit upon other devices to impose on a people. But he who knows nothing more, though he may be lucky enough to get together an assembly of fools and madmen, will never lay the foundations of an Empire; the fabrick raised by his extravagance presently falling and often burying him in its ruins. A transitory union may be formed from slight and futile connections; nothing but the dictates of wisdom, however, can render it durable. The Jewish law, still subsisting, and that of the son of Ismael, which for ten centuries hath governed half the world, are standing proofs of the superior genius of those great men by whom they were dictated: and though the vanity of philosophy, and the blind prejudice of party see nothing in their characters but fortunate impostors, the true politician admires, in their respective institutions, that sagacious and comprehensive power of mind which must ever lay the lasting foundation of human establishments.

It must not, from all this, be concluded, however, that religion and government have, in our times, as Warburton alleges, one common object; but only that in the first establishment of societies, the one was made instrumental to the other.   C H A P.

C H A P. VIII.

Of the people.

AS the architect, before he begins to raise an edifice, examines into the ground where he is to lay the foundation, that he may be able to judge whether it will bear the weight of the superstructure; so the prudent legiflator does not begin by making a digest of falutary laws, but examines first whether the people for whom fuch laws are defigned, are capable of fupporting them. It was for this reafon Plato refufed to give laws to the Arcadians and Cyrenians, knowing they were rich and luxurious, and could not admit of the introduction of equality among them. It was for this reafon that Crete, though it boafted good laws, was inhabited by fuch bad men; Minos had only endeavoured to govern a people already depraved by vice. Various have been the nations that have made a diftinguifhed figure in the world, and yet have not been capable of being governed by good laws; and even thofe who were capable of being fo governed, continued fo but a fhort time. Nations, as well as individuals, are docile only in their infancy: they be-

become incorrigible as they grow old. When
cuſtoms are once eſtabliſhed and prejudices
have taken root among them, it is a dangerous and fruitlefs enterprize to attempt to re-
form them. A people cannot even bear to have
their wounds probed, though in order to be
cured ; but refemble thofe weak and cowardly
patients who ſhudder at the fight of their phyfician. Not, but that fometimes, as there are
diftempers which affect the brain of individuals
and deprive them of the capacity of remember-
ing what is paft, there happen in ſtates fuch
revolutions as produce the fame effect on a people, when the horror of the paft fupplies the
place of oblivion, and the ftate, inflamed and
exhaufted by civil wars, rifes again, if I may
fo exprefs myfelf, out of its own aſhes, and re-
affumes the vigour of youth in forfaking the
arms of death. This was the cafe with Sparta
in the time of Lycurgus, and of Rome after the
Tarquins; and fuch hath been the cafe in modern times with Holland and Switzerland after
the expulfion of their tyrants. But thefe events
are rare ; and are fuch exceptions as have their
caufe in the particular conftitution of the ftate
excepted. They cannot even take place twice
among the fame people : for though they may
be made free when they are only barbarous and
un-

uncivilized; yet, when the refources of fociety are exhaufted, they cannot be renewed. In that cafe, faction may deftroy, but revolutions cannot re-eftablifh their freedom; they require for ever after a mafter, and not a deliverer. Every free people, therefore, fhould remember this maxim, that tho' nations may acquire liberty, yet if once this ineftimable acquifition is loft, it is abfolutely irrecoverable.

There is in nations, as well as individuals, a term of maturity, at which they fhould be permitted to arrive before they are fubjected to laws. This term, however, is not always eafy to be known; and yet if it be anticipated it may be of dangerous confequence. Again, one people may be formed to difcipline in their infancy; while another may not be ripened for fubjection till after many centuries. The Ruffians, for inftance, will never be truly polifhed becaufe they were difciplined too foon. Peter had only an imitative turn; he had nothing of that true genius, whofe creative power forms things out of nothing. Some of his meafures, indeed, were proper enough, but moft of them were ill-timed or ill-placed. He faw that his fubjects were mere barbarians, but he did not

fee

fee that they were not ripe for being made polite. He wanted to civilize them, when he should
only have checked their brutality. He wanted
to make them, at once, Germans and Englifh-
men, whereas he ought to have begun by
making them firft Ruffians; and thus he prevented his fubjects from ever becoming what
otherwife they might have been, by per-
fuading them they were fuch as they were
not. It is thus a French tutor forms his pupil
to make a figure in his child-hood, and to
make none for ever afterwards. The Empire
of Ruffia, while it is ambitious of reducing all
Europe to its fubjection, will be fubjected
itfelf. Its neighbours, the Tartars, will in time
become both its mafters and ours. This event
feems to me inevitable; all the monarchs in
Europe feeming to act, in concert, to accelerate
fuch a revolution.

C H A P. IX.

The fubject continued.

IN the fame manner as nature hath limited
the dimenfions of a well-formed human
body, beyond which fhe produces only giants
or dwarfs, fo in the body politic there are
limits,

limits, within or beyond which a ftate ought not to be confined or extended; to the end that it may not be too big to be well governed, nor too little to maintain its own independency. There is in every body politic a *maximum* of force which it cannot exceed, and from which it often recedes by extending its dominion. The more the focial knot is extended, the more lax it grows; and in general, a little ftate is always proportionably ftronger than a great one.

A thoufand reafons might be given in fupport of this maxim. In the firft place, the adminiftration of government becomes always more difficult as the diftance from the feat of it in-creafes, even as a body has the greateft weight at the end of the longeft lever. It be-comes alfo more burthenfome in proportion as it is divided into parts; for every town hath firft its own particular government to pay; that of each diftrict again is paid by the fame people; next that of the province, then that of particular governments with their viceroys, all of whom are to be paid as they rife in dignity, and always at the expence of the unhappy people; whom, laft of all, the fupreme adminiftration itfelf crufhes with the whole weight of its oppreffion. It is impoffible fo many

E

need-

needlefs charges fhould not tend continually
to impoverifh the people; who, fo far from
being better governed by thefe different ranks
of fuperiors, are much worfe fo, than if they
had but one order of governors in the ftate.
And yet with this multiplicity of rulers, they
are far from being furnifhed with proper refources for extraordinary occafions; but, on
the contrary, when they have occafion to recur
to them, the ftate is always on the brink of
ruin.

Nor is this all; the government not only becomes lefs vigorous and active in putting the
laws in execution, removing private oppreffion,
correcting abufes, or preventing the feditious
enterprifes of rebellion in diftant provinces;
but the people have lefs affection for their chiefs,
whom they never have an opportunity to fee;
for their country, which to them is like the
whole world; and for their fellow-fubjects, of
which the greater part are utter ftrangers. The
fame laws cannot be convenient for fo many
various people of different manners, and climates, and who cannot be fuppofed to live
equally happy under the fame form of government. And yet different laws muft occafion
much

much trouble and confusion among people,
who, living under the same adminiftration, and
carrying on a perpetual intercourfe, frequently
change their habitations, inter-marry with each
other, and, being educated under different cuftoms, hardly ever know when their property
is fecure. Great talents lie buried, virtue lives
obfcured, and vice prevails with impunity, amidft
that multitude of ftrangers, which flock together round the chief feat of adminiftration.
The principals, overwhelmed with a multiplicity of bufinefs, can look into nothing themfelves; the government of the ftate being left
to their deputies and clerks. In a word, the
meafures to be taken, in order to maintain the
general authority, on which fo many diftant
officers are ever ready to encroach or impofe,
engrofs the public attention; there is none of
it left to be employed about the happinefs of
the people, and indeed hardly any for their defence in cafe of need: thus it is, that a body too
unwieldy for its conftitution grows debilitated
and finks under its own weight.

On the other hand, a ftate ought to be fixed
on fome bafis, to fecure its folidity, to be able
to refift thofe fhocks which it will not fail to
encounter, and to make thofe efforts which it

E 2   will

will find neceffary to maintain its independence.
Nations have all a kind of centrifugal force by
which they act continually againft each other,
and tend, like the vortices of Defcartes, to aggran-
dize themfelves at the expence of their neighbours.   Thus the weak run in danger of being
prefently fwallowed up by the ftrong ; nor is
there any fecurity for them, but by keeping
themfelves in equilibrio with the reft, and making the compreffion on every fide equal.

Hence we fee it is prudent in fome cafes to
extend, and in others to reftrain, the limits of a
ftate ; nor is it one of the leaft arts in civil polity to diftinguifh between one and the other,
and to fix on that advantageous proportion
which tends moft to the prefervation of the
ftate.   It may be obferved in general, that the
reafons for extending dominion, relating to objects external and relative, ought to be fubordinate to thofe for contracting it, whofe objects
are internal and abfolute.   A found and vigorous
conftitution is the firft thing to be confidered,
and a much greater reliance is to be made on a
good government, than on the refources which
are to be drawn from an extenfive territory.

Not

Not but that there have been inftances of ftates fo conftituted, that the neceffity of their making conquefts hath been effential to their very conftitution. It is poffible alfo they might felicitate themfelves on that happy neceffity, which pointed out, neverthelefs, with the fummit of their grandeur, the inevitable moment of their fall.

C H A P. X.

The fubject continued.

THE magnitude of a body politic may be taken two ways; viz. by the extent of territory, and the number of the people; a certain proportional relation between them conftituting the real greatnefs of a ftate. It is the people which form the ftate, and the territory which affords fubfiftence to the people; this relation, therefore, exifts when the territory is fufficient for the fubfiftence of the inhabitants, and the inhabitants are as numerous as the territory can maintain. In this proportion confifts the *maximum* of the force of any given number of people; for if the territory be too extenfive, the defence of it is burthenfome, the cultivation infufficient, and the produce fuper-

E 3   fluous;

fluous; hence the proximate caufes of defenfive war. If, on the other hand, the territory be too fmall, the ftate is under the neceffity of being obliged for part of its fubfiftence to its neighbours; hence the proximate caufes of offenfive war. Every people who, by their fituation, have no other alternative than commerce or war, muft be neceffarily feeble: they muft depend on their neighbours, on adventitious circumftances, and can only have a fhort and uncertain exiftence. They muft conquer others, and thereby change their fituation, or be conquered themfelves, and thence be reduced to nothing. It is impoffible fuch a ftate can preferve its independency but by its infignificancy or its greatnefs.

It is not eafy to calculate the determinate relation between the extent of territory and number of inhabitants, fufficient for each other; not only on account of the difference in the qualities of the foil, in its degrees of fertility, in the nature of its productions, and in the influence of climate, but alfo on account of the remarkable difference in the temperament and conftitution of the inhabitants; fome confuming but little in a fertile country, and others a great deal on a barren foil. Regard muft alfo be had to
the

the degree of fecundity among the females, to the circumstances favourable or destructive to population, and to the number of people which the legislator may hope to draw from other countries by the advantages attending his scheme of government; so that he ought not to found his judgment on what actually exists; but on what he foresees may exist here-after; not on the present state of population, but on that which will naturally succeed. In fine, there are a thousand occasions, on which local accidents acquire, or permit, a state to possess a larger share of territory than may appear actually necessary for present use. Thus a people may spread themselves over a large spot in a mountainous country, whose natural produce, of wood or pasture, requires less labour of cultivation; where experience teaches us that women are more fruitful than in the flat countries; and in which a large inclined superficies gives but a small horizontal base, by which only the land must be estimated in the affair of vegetation. A people, on the contrary, may inhabit a less space on the sea-shore, or even a-mong rocks and almost barren sands; because the fishery supplies them with sustenance, instead of the produce of the earth; they can easily disburthen their community by sending

E 4 out

out colonies of its supernumerary inhabitants; and lastly, because it is necessary for them in such a case to live near to each other, in order to repel the invasions of pyrates.

We may add to these conditional precautions, respecting the formation of a people, one that can be supplied by no other, but without which all the rest are useless: this is, that they should enjoy peace and plenty. For the time in which a state is forming, resembles that in which soldiers are forming a battalion; it is the moment in which they are least capable of resistance, and the most easily defeated. They would even make a greater resistance when put into absolute disorder afterwards, than during the interval of their first fermentation, when each is taken up more about his own particular rank than the common danger. Should a war, a famine, or a rebellion, break out at such a crisis, the state would be infallibly subverted.

Not but there have been many governments established in times of disorder and confusion: in such cases, however, those very governments subverted the state. Usurpers have always given rise to, or took the advantage of, those times of general confusion, in order

der to procure fuch deftructive laws, which the people never could have been prevailed on to pafs at a more difpaffionate feafon. The choice of the proper time for the inftitution of laws, is one of the moft certain tokens by which we may diftinguifh the defign of a legiflator from that of a tyrant.

If it be afked then, what people are in a fituation to receive a fyftem of laws? I anfwer, thofe who, though connected by fome primitive union either of intereft or compact, are not yet truly fubjected to regular laws; thofe whofe cuftoms and prejudices are not deeply rooted; thofe who are under no fear of being fwallowed up by a fudden invafion, and who, without entering into the quarrels of their neighbours, are able to encounter feparately with each, or to engage the affiftance of one to repel the other; a people whofe individuals may be known to each other, and among whom it is not necef-fary to charge a man with a greater burthen than it is poffible for him to bear; a people who can fubfift without others, and without whom all others might fubfift *; a people nei-ther

* If two neighbouring people were fo fituated that one could not fubfift without the other, the circum-

ther rich nor poor, but poſſeſſed of a compe-
tence within themſelves; a people, in ſhort,
who poſſeſs at once the conſiſtency of an ancient nation, and the docility of a newly-created
one.   The great difficulty in legiſlation, con-
ſiſts leſs in knowing what ought to be eſtabliſhed
than what ought to be eradicated ; and what
renders it ſo ſeldom ſuccefsful, is the impoſſibi-
lity of finding the ſimplicity of nature in the
wants of ſociety.   It is true that all theſe circumſtances are very rarely united ; and it is for
this reaſon that ſo few ſtates have much to
boaſt of, in their conſtitution.   There is ſtill
one country in Europe capable of receiving
laws : this is the iſland of Corſica.   The valour and conſtancy, with which thoſe brave
people recovered, and have defended their liber-

ſtances of the firſt would be very hard, and of the latter
very dangerous.   Every wiſe nation, in ſuch a caſe,
would extricate itſelf as ſoon as poſſible from ſuch
a ſtate of dependence.   The republic of Thlaſcala,
ſituated in the heart of the Mexican empire, choſe
rather to be without ſalt than purchaſe it, or even
receive it gratis of the Mexicans.   The prudent
Thlaſcalans ſaw through the ſnare of ſuch liberality.
Thus they preſerved their liberty ; this petty ſtate,
included within that great empire, being, in the end,
the cauſe of its ruin.

ty,

ty, might defervedly excite fome wife man to teach them how to preferve it. I cannot help furmifing, that this little ifland will, one day or other, be the aftonifhment of Europe.

CHAP. XI.

Of the various fyftems of legiflature.

IF we were to enquire, in what confifts pre-cifely the greateft good, or what ought to be the end of every fyftem of legiflature; we fhould find it reducible to two principal ob-jects, *liberty* and *equality*; liberty, becaufe all .partial dependence deprives the whole body of the ftate of fo much ftrength; equality, be-caufe liberty cannot fubfift without it.

I have already explained the nature of focial liberty; and with regard to equality, we are not to underftand by that term, that individuals fhould all abfolutely poffefs the fame degree of wealth and power; but only that, with refpect to the latter, it fhould never be exercifed con-trary to good order and the laws; and with refpect to the former, that no one citizen fhould be rich enough to buy another, and that none fhould be fo poor as to be obliged to fell him-

E 6   felf,

felf*. This fuppofes a moderation of poffeffion
and credit on the fide of the great, and the moderation of defires and covetoufnefs on the part
of the little.

This equality, they tell us, is a mere fpecu-
lative chimera, which cannot exift in practice
but though abufes are inevitable, does it thence
follow they are not to be corrected ? It is for the
very reafon that things always tend to deftroy
this equality, that the laws fhould be calculated
to preferve it.

Thefe general objects of legiflature, how-
cver, fhould be varioufly modified in different
countries, agreeable to local fituation, the character of the inhabitants, and thofe other circumftances which require that every people
fhould have a particular fyftem of laws, not
always the beft in itfelf, but the beft adapted to

* Would you give a ftate confiftency and ftrength,
prevent the two extremes as much as poffible ; let
there be no rich perfons nor beggars. Thefe two
conditions, naturally infeparable, are equally deftructive to the commonwealth : the one furnifhes tyrants,
and the other the fupporters of tyranny. It is by
thefe the traffic of public liberty is carried on ; the
one buying, the other felling it.

that

that ftate for which it is calculated. If, for example, the foil be ungrateful and barren, or the country too fmall for its inhabitants, cherifh induftry and the arts, the produ&ions of which may be exchanged for the commodities required. On the other hand, if your country abounds in fertile hills and plenteous vales; if you live on a rich foil in want of inhabitants; apply yourfelves to agriculture, which affords the means of population ; and banifh the deftru&ive arts which ferve only to ruin a country, by gathering the few inhabitants of ir, together in one particular fpot or two, to the depopulation of all the reft *. Do you occupy an extenfive and commodious fituation by the fea fide ? Cover the ocean with your fhips, cultivate the arts of navigation and commerce : you will by thefe means enjoy a brilliant but fhort exiftence. On the contrary, do the waves only wafte their ftrength againft your inacceffibie rocks ? Remain barbarous and illiterate ; you will live out the more at eafe, perhaps more virtuous, af-

* The advantage of foreign commerce, fays the Marquis d'A. is produ&ive only of a delufive util.ty to the kingdom in general. It may enrich a few individuals, and perhaps fome cities; but the whole nation gains nothing by it, nor are the people the better for it.

furedly ·

furedly more happy. In a word, befides the
maxims common to all nations, every people
are poffeffed in themfelves of fome caufe which
influences them in a particular manner, and
renders their own fyftem of laws proper only
for themfelves. It is thus that in ancient times,
among the Hebrews, and in modern times, a-
mong the Arabians, religion was made the principal object of national concern; among the
Athenians this object was literature; at Car-
thage and Tyre it was commerce, at Rhodes it
was navigation, at Sparta war, and at Rome
public virtue. The author of the *Spirit of laws*
hath fhewn, by a number of examples, in what
manner the legiflator fhould model his fyftem
agreeable to each of thefe objects.

What renders the conftitution of a ftate truly
folid and durable, is that agreement maintained
therein between natural and focial relations,
which occafions the legiflature always to act in
concert with nature, while the laws ferve only
to confirm and rectify, as it were, the dictates
of the former. But if the legiflator, deceived
in his object, fhould affume a principle different
from that which arifes from the nature of things;
fhould the one tend to flavery and the other to
liberty, one to riches, the other to population,

one

one to peace the other to war and conquefts, the laws would infenfibly lofe their force, the conftitution would alter, and the ftate continue to be agitated till it fhould be totally changed or deftroyed, and nature have refumed its empire.

CHAP. XII.

On the divifion of the laws.

IN order to provide for the government of the whole, or give the beft poffible form to the conftitution, various circumftances are to be taken into confideration. Of thefe the firft is the action of the whole body operating on it-felf; that is the relation of the whole to the whole, or of the fovereign to the ftate, which relation is compofed of thofe between the inter-mediate terms; as will be feen hereafter.

The laws which govern this relation bear the name of politic laws, and are alfo called funda-mental laws, not without fome reafon when they are wifely ordained. For if there be only one good method of government in a ftate, the peo-ple, who have been fo happy as to hit on that method, ought to abide by it: but, wherefore

4 'fhould

fhould a people, whofe laws are bad or defective, efteem fuch laws to be fundamental? Befides, a nation is in any cafe at liberty to change
even the beft laws, when it pleafes: for if a
people have a mind even to do themfelves an
injury, who hath any right to prevent them?

The fecond circumftance is the relations
which the members of the community bear to
each other and to the whole body, the firft of
which fhould be as little, and the laft as great,
as poffible : fo that every citizen fhould live in a
ftate of perfect independence on all the reft,
and in a ftate of the greateft dependence on the
city. Both thefe are ever effected by the fame
means : for it is the power of the ftate only
that conftitutes the liberty of its members. On
this fecond kind of relation is laid the immediate
foundation of the civil laws.

It may be proper to confider alfo a third
fpecies of relation between the individual and
the law ; which gives immediate rife to penal
ftatutes : thefe, however, are in fact lefs a diftinct fpecies of laws than the fanction of all
the others.

To

To thefe three kinds of laws, may be added a fourth, more important than all the reft ; and which are neither engraven on brafs or marble ; but in the hearts of the citizens ; forming the real conftitution of the ftate. Thefe are the laws which acquire daily frefh influence, and when others grow old and obfolete, invigorate and revive them : thefe are the laws which keep alive in the hearts of the people, the original fpirit of their inftitution, and fubftitute infenfibly the force. of habit to that of authority. The laws I here fpeak of, are manners, cuftoms, and above all public opinion ; all unknown or difregarded by our modern politicians, but on which depends the fuccefs of all the reft. Thefe are the objects on which the real legiflator is employed in fecret, while he appears folely to confine himfelf to thofe particular regulations which compofe only the preparatory centre of the vault, of which manners, more flow in their progrefs, form in the end the immoveable arch.

Of thefe claffes, politic laws, or thofe which conftitute the form of government, are relative only to my prefent fubject.

The END of the SECOND BOOK.

BOOK

BOOK III.

BEFORE we enter on a difcuffion of the feveral forms of government, it will not be improper to afcertain the precife meaning of that term; which as yet hath not been well explained.

CHAP. I.

On government in general.

I MUST previoufly caution the reader to perufe this chapter very deliberately, as it is impoffible to render myfelf clearly intelligible to fuch as are not attentive.

Every free action hath two caufes, which concur to effect its production, the one moral, viz. the will which determines the act; the other phyfical, viz. the power which puts it in execution. When I walk, for inftance, toward any particular object, it is firft neceffary that I fhould will to go; and fecondly that my feet fhould bear me forward. A paralytic may will to run, and an active racer be unwilling; the want of power in the one hath the fame effect

as

as the want of will in the other; both remain
in their place. The body politic hath the fame
principles of motion; which are diftinguifhed
alfo in the fame manner by power and will:
the latter under the name of the *legiſlative*
power, and the former under that of the *executive*
power. Nothing is or ought to be done
without the concurrence of both.

We have already feen that the legiflative
power belongs to the people in general, and can
belong to none elfe. On the other hand,
it is eafy to conclude, from the principles already eftablifhed, that the executive power cannot appertain to the generality, as legiflator
or fovereign; becaufe this power is exerted only
in particular acts which are not the province of
the law, nor of courfe that of the fovereign,
whofe acts can be no other than laws.

To the public force, therefore, fhould be
annexed a proper agent, which may re-unite
and put it in action, agreeable to the directions
of the general will; ferving as a communication between the ftate and the fovereign, and
effecting the fame purpofe in the body politic,
as the union of the foul and body in man. Such
is the rationale of government, fo generally confounded

founded with the sovereign, of which it is only the miniftry.

What then is government? It is an interme-diate body eftablifhed between the fubject and the fovereign, for their mutual correfpondence; charged with the execution of the laws, and with the maintenance of civil and political liberty.

The members of which this body is compof-ed, are called magiftrates or *kings*, that is to fay, *governors*, and the whole body bears the name of the *prince* *. Thofe, therefore, who affirm that the act, by which a people profefs fubmiffion to their chiefs or governors, is not a contract, are certainly right; it being in fact nothing more than the conferring a fimple com-miffion on the faid chiefs; an employ, in the difcharge of which they act as mere officers of the fovereign, exercifing in its name the power which it hath placed in their hands, and which it may limit, modify or refume whenever it pleafes; the alienation of its right fo to do, being incompatible with the very nature and being of fociety.

* Thus at Venice the college of fenators is called the moft ferene *prince*, even when the doge is not prefent.

I call

I call therefore, the legal exercife of the executive power, the *Government* or fupreme adminiftration; and the individual or body, charged with that adminiftration, the prince or the magiftrate.

In the government are to be found thofe intermediate forces, whofe relations compofe that of the whole to the whole, or of the fovereign to the ftate. This laft relation may be reprefented by that of the extremes of a conftant proportion, the mean proportional of which is the government. The government receives from the fovereign thofe orders, which it gives to the people; fo that, in order to keep the ftate in due equilibrio, there fhould, every thing confidered, be the fame equality between the momentum or force of the government taken in itfelf, and the momentum or force of the citizens, who are the fovereign confidered collectively on one fide, and fubjects confidered feverally on the other.

It is, befides, impoffible to vary any of thefe three terms, without inftantly deftroying the proportions. If the fovereign fhould be defirous to govern, or the magiftrate to give laws, or the fubjects refufe to obey; diforder muft im-

me-

mediately take place; the will and the power thus no longer acting in concert, the state would be dissolved, and fall into despotism or anarchy. Add to this, that as there can be but one mean proportional between each relation, there can be but one good government for a state. But as a thousand events may change the relations subsisting among a people; different governments may not only be good for different people, but even for the same people at different periods of time.

In order to give the reader an idea of the various relations that may exist between these two extremes, I shall, by way of example, make use of the number of people, as a relation the most easily expressed.

We will suppose, for instance, that a state is composed of ten thousand citizens. The sovereign must be considered as collectively only and in a body: but every particular in quality of subject is considered as an individual: thus the sovereign is in this case to the subject as ten thousand to one: That is to say, every member of the state shares only the ten thousandth part of the sovereign authority, while at the same time he is subjected to it in his whole person. Again, should the number of people be increased

to

to an hundred thoufand, the fubmiffion of the
fubjects would receive no alteration; each of
them being totally fubjected to the authority of
the laws, while his fhare in the fovereignty,
and vote in the enaction of thefe laws, would
be reduced to the hundred-thoufandth part; a
tenth lefs than before. Thus the fubject, remaining always a fingle integer, the proportion
between him and the fovereign increafes as the
number of citizens is augmented: whence it
follows, that as a ftate increafes, the liberty
of the fubject diminifhes.

When I fay the proportion increafes, I mean
that it recedes farther from the point of equality. Thus the greater the proportion, in the
language of the geometricians, it is reckoned
the lefs according to common acceptation: a-
greeable to the former, the relation, confidered
in point of quantity, is eftimated by its extent;
and according to the latter, confidered in point
of identity, it is eftimated by its proxima-
tion.

Now, the lefs proportion which particular
voices bear to the general, that is to fay, the
manners to the laws, the more ought the general reftrictive force to be augmented. Thus the
government fhould be relatively more powerful
as the people are more numerous.

On

On the other hand, the increafing greatnefs
of a ftate affording the guardians of the public authority greater temptations and means to
abufe their power, the more force a government is poffeffed of to reftrain the people, the
more ought the fovereign to be poffeffed of in
its turn to reftrain the government. I am not
fpeaking here of abfolute power, but of the
·relative forces of the component parts of the
ftate.

It follows, from this two-fold relation, that
the conftant proportion between the fovereign,
the prince, and the people, is not a mere arbitrary idea, but a neceffary confequence of the
very exiftence of the body politic. It follows
alfo, that, one of the extremes, *viz.* the people
as fubjects, being a fixed term reprefented by
unity, wherever the two-fold ratio is increafed
or diminifhed, that the fimple ratio muft increafe or diminifh in like manner, and of courfe
the mean term will be changed. Hence it appears there is no one fettled conftitution of government, but that there may be as many governments different in their nature as there are
ftates differing in magnitude.

If

If any one fhould affect to turn my fyftem into ridicule, and fay that, in order to find this mean proportional, and form the government as it ought to be, we have no more to do than to find the fquare root of the number of the people; I anfwer that I here make ufe of the number of people only by way of example; that the relations of which I have been fpeaking, are not only eftimated by the number of individuals, but in general by the momentum or quantity of action, which arifes from a combination of various caufes; and though, in order to exprefs myfelf concifely, I borrow the terms of geometry, I am not ignorant that geometrical precifion is not to be expected in treating of moral quantities.

The government is in miniature what the body politic containing it, is at large. It is a moral perfon endued with certain faculties, active as the fovereign, paffive as the ftate, and capable of being refolved into other fenfible relations, from which of courfe arifes a new fcale of proportion, and ftill another within this, according to the order of the courts of juftice, till we arrive at the laft indivifible term, that is to fay, the fole chief or fupreme magiftrate, which may be reprefented in the centre

F   of

of this progreſſion, as an unity between the
ſeries of fractions, and that of whole numbers.

But, without embarraſſing the reader with a
multiplicity of terms, we ſhall content ourſelves
with conſidering the government as a new body
in the ſtate, diſtinct from the ſubjects and the
ſovereign, and exiſting between both.

There is this eſſential difference, however,
between the government and the ſtate, that the
latter exiſts of itſelf, and the former only by
means of the ſovereign. Thus as the ruling
will of the prince is, or ought to be, only the
general will, or the law, the power of the
prince is only that of the public centered in
him ; ſo that whenever he would derive from
himſelf any abſolute and independent act, the
combination of the whole is affected. And if,
at length, the prince ſhould have a particular
will of his own, more active than that of the .
ſovereign, and ſhould make uſe of the public
power in his hands to enforce obedience to ſuch
particular will, forming, as it were, two ſovereigns, the one of right and the other of
fact, the ſocial union immediately vaniſhes, and
the body politic is diſſolved.

In

In order that the body of government, neverthelefs, may have an exiftence, a real life to diftinguifh it from that of the ftate, and that its members
may act in concert to anfwer the end for which
it is inftituted, it is neceffary that it fhould be
poffeffed of a particular identity, a fenfibility
common to all its members, a power and will
of its own for the fake of its prefervation. Such
a particular exiftence neceffarily fuppofes that
of affemblies and councils ; of a power to deliberate and refolve; of the rights, titles and
privileges which belong exclufively to the
prince, and render the fituation of a magiftrate
the more honourable in proportion as it is
more laborious. The difficulty lies in the method of difpofing all the inferior parts of the
whole body ; fo that, while it is ftrengthening
its own conftitution, it may not injure that of
the ftate. At the fame time alfo, it fhould
always diftinguifh between the peculiar force,
deftined to its own prefervation, and the public
force deftined to the prefervation of the ftate ;
in a word, it fhould be always ready to facrifice the government to the people, and not the
people to the government.

To this we may add, that, although the artificial body of government be the work of an-

other

other artificial body, and is poffeffed only of a
borrowed and fubordinate exiftence ; this doth
not prevent it from acting with different degrees
of vigour and celerity, or from enjoying, if I
may fo exprefs myfelf, a greater or lefs fhare
of health and ftrength.   In fhort, it may, without running diametrically oppofite to the purpofes of its inftitution, deviate from them more
or lefs, according to the mode in which it is
conftituted.

It is from all thefe differences that arife thofe
various relations and proportions, which the government ought to bear toward the ftate, according to thefe accidental and particular relations in which the ftate is modified.   For the
beft government in itfelf may often become the
worft, if the relation of its component parts
are not altered according to the defects of the
body politic to which it belongs.

C H A P.

CHAP. II.

On the principle whi.h conflitutes the different forms of government.

TO explain the general caufe of thefe differences, it is neceffary to diftinguifh here between the prince and the government, in the fame manner as I have already done between the fovereign and the ftate. The body of the magiftracy may be compofed of a greater or a lefs number of members. It hath been obferved alfo that the relation the fovereign bears to the fubject increafes in proportion to the number of people; thus, by an evident analogy, we may fay the fame of the relation between the government and the magiftrates.

Now the total force of the government, being always equal to that of the ftate, fuffers no alteration; whence it follows that the more fuch force is fpent by the diftribution of it among the members of the government, the lefs remains to be exerted on the whole body of people.

F 3. That

That government, therefore, which is in the hands of the greateft number of magiftrates muft, be the moft feeble.   As this is a fundamental maxim, we fhall take fome pains to illuftrate it.

In the perfon of the magiftrate may be diftinguifhed three wills effentially different.   In the firft place the particular will of the individual, which tends only to his private advantage ; fecondly, that will which is common to him as a magiftrate, tending folely to the advantage of the prince ; being general with refpe& to the government, and particular with regard to the ftate, of which the government is only a part ; and in the third place, the will of the people or the fovereign will, which is general as well with regard to the ftate confidered as a whole, as with regard to the government confidered as a part of that whole.

In a compleat fyftem of legiflature, the particular will or that of the individual fhould amount to nothing; the will of the body of government fhould be very limited, and of courfe the general or fovereign will the ruling and fole dire&or of all the others.

Ac-

According to the order of nature, however, thefe different wills are ranged in a contrary manner; being always- more active as they are concentrated in themfelves. Thus the general will is always the moft feeble, that of the government next, and the will of the individual the ftrongeft of all ; fo that each member of the adminiftration is to be confidered firft of all as an individual, fecondly as a magiftrate, and laftly as a citizen: a gradation directly oppofite to that which the order of fociety requires.

This point being fettled, let us fuppofe the adminiftration of government committed to the hands of one man. In this cafe the will of the individual, and that of the body of the magiftracy are perfectly united, and of confequence the latter poffeffes the greateft degree of intenfity. Now, as it is on the degree of the will that the exertion of force depends, and as the abfolute force of the government never varies, it follows that the moft active of all adminiftrations muft be that of a fingle perfon.

On the contrary, if we unite the adminiftration and the legiflature; if we make the prince

F 4   the

the sovereign, and the citizens all so many magiftrates: in this cafe, the will of the government, confounded with the general will, would
poffefs no greater fhare of activity, but would
leave the particular will of individuals to exert
its whole force. Thus the government, having always the fame degree of abfolute force,
would be at its *minimum* of relative force or
activity.

Thefe relations are inconteftible, and may be
farther confirmed by other confiderations. It
is evident, for example, that the magiftrate is
more active in that capacity than the citizen in
his, and that of courfe the will of the individual muft have a more confiderable fhare of influence in the adminiftration of government,
than in the actions of the fovereign ; every
magiftrate being almoft always charged with
fome function of government, whereas no citizen, confidered as an individual, difcharges
any function of the fovereignty. Befide this,
the real force of a ftate increafes, as the ftate
increafes in magnitude, though not always in
the ratio of that magnitude ; but while the
ftate remains the fame, it is in vain to increafe
the number of magiftrates, as the government
will not thereby acquire any additional ftrength,
                                                becaufe

becaufe its force, being always that of the ftate, is conftantly equal. And thus the relative force or activity of government is diminifhed, without its real and abfolute force being augmented.

It is farther certain that public affairs muft be tranfacted more or lefs expeditioufly according to the number of people, charged with their difpatch ; that by laying too great a ftrefs on prudence, too little is trufted to fortune ; that the opportunity of fuccefs is thus frequently loft, and that by the mere force of deliberation the end of it is defeated.

This may ferve to prove that the reins of government are relaxed in proportion as the magiftrates are multiplied ; and I have before demonftrated that the more numerous the people are, the more fhould the reftraining power of government be increafed : Hence it follows that the proportion which the number of magiftrates fhould hold to the government fhould be in the inverfe ratio of the fubjects to the fovereign ; that is to fay, the more extenfive the ftate the more contracted fhould be the government, the number of chiefs diminifhing as that of the people increafes.

F 5.   I fpeak

I fpeak here only of the relative force of the government, and not of the rectitude or propriety of it.   For, otherwife, it is certain that the more numerous the magiftracy is, the nearer doth the will of that body approach to the general will of the whole people ; whereas under a fole chief, the will of the magiftracy is, as I have before obferved, only that of an individual.   Thus what is gained in one refpect, is loft on the other ; and the art of the legiflator confifts in tracing the fixed point, at which the force and the will of the government, always in a reciprocal proportion to each other, unite in that proportion which is moft advantageous to the ftate.

C H A P.   III.

Of the actual diftinctions of governments.

WE have treated in the preceding chapter of the reafons for diftinguifhing the feveral fpecies and forms of government, by the number of the members compofing them ; it remains therefore to fhew, in the prefent, how thefe diftinctions are actually made.

The

The fovereign authority may, in the firft place, commit the charge of the government to the whole people or to the greater part of them ; the number of magiftrates in fuch cafe exceeding that of private citizens. This form of government is diftinguifhed by the name of a democracy.

Or, otherwife, the fupreme power may commit the office of government into the hands of a few, fo that the number of private citizens may exceed that of magiftrates ; and this form bears the name of an ariftocracy.

Or laftly, the government may be entrufted to one magiftrate only, who delegates his power to all the reft. This third form is the moft common, and is called a monarchy or a regal government.

It is to be obferved that all thefe forms, and particularly the two former, are fufceptible of different degrees of perfection, and admit indeed of confiderable latitude in their modification : for a democracy may comprehend the whole people, or be limited to the half. An ariftocracy alfo may comprehend any quantity

· F 6   from

from the half of the people to the smallest
number indefinitely. Nay a monarchy itself is
susceptible of some distribution. Sparta, for
instance, had constitutionally two kings at a
time; and the Romans had even eight emperors
at once, without the empire having been actually divided. Thus, we see, there is a certain point, at which each form of government
is confounded with that to which it is nearest re-
lated; and thus under three distinguishing de-
nominations only, government is really susceptible of as many different forms, as there are
citizens in the state.

To go still farther; as even one and the same
government is capable, in many respects, of being
subdivided into parts, of which the administration may respectively differ, there may result
from the varied combinations of these forms a
multitude of others, every one of which may
be again multiplied by all the simple forms.

Politicians have in all ages disputed much
about the best form of government, without
considering that each different form may pos-
sibly be the best in some cases, and the worst in
others.

If

If in diffcrent ftates the number of fupreme magiftrates fhould be in the inverfe ratio to that of the citizens, it follows that the democratical government is generally fpeaking better fuited to fmall ftates, the ariftocratical to middling ftates, and the monarchical to great ftates. This rule is deduced immediately from our principles; but it is impoffible to particularize the multiplicity of circumftances which may furnifh exceptions againft it.

CHAP. IV.

Of a Democracy.

THE inftitutor of a law fhould certainly know better than any other perfon, how it ought to be underftood and executed. It fhould feem therefore that the beft conftitution, muft be that in which the legiflative and executive powers are lodged in the fame hands. It is this very circumftance, however, that renders fuch a government imperfect; becaufe there doth not exift the neceffary diftinction, which ought to be made in its parts; while the prince and the fovereign, being one and the fame perfon, only form, if I may fo exprefs myfelf, a government without a government.

It

It is not proper that the power which makes the laws fhould execute them, or that the attention of the whole body of the people fhould be diverted from-general views to particular objects. Nothing is more,dangerous than the influence of private intereft in publick affairs; the abufe of the laws by the government, being a lefs evil than the corruption of the legiflature; which is infallibly the confequence of its being governed by particular views. For in that cafe, the ftate being effentially altered, all reformation becomes impoffible. A people who would not abufe the power of government, would be no more propenfe to abufe their independence; and a people who fhould always govern well, would have no occafion to be governed at all.

To take the term in its ftricteft fenfe, there never exifted, and never will exift, a real democracy in the world. It is contrary to the natural order of things, that the majority of a people fhould be the governors, and the minority the governed. It is not to be conceived that a whole people fhould remain perfonally affembled to manage the affairs of the public; and it is evident, that no fooner are deputies or reprefentatives appointed, than the form of the adminiftration is changed.

It.

It may be laid down indeed as a maxim, that when the functions of government are divided among several courts, that which is compofed of the feweft perfons will, fooner or later, acquire the greateft authority ; though it were for no other reafon than the facility with which it is calculated to expedite affairs.

Such a form of government fuppofes, alfo, the concurrence of a number of circumftances rarely united. In the firft place, it is requifite that the ftate itfelf fhould be of fmall extent, fo that the people might be eafily affembled and all perfonally known to each other. Secondly, the fimplicity of their manners fhould be fuch as to prevent a multiplicity of affairs, and per-plexity in difcuffing them : And thirdly, there fhould fubfift a great degree of equality between the rank and fortunes of individuals ; without which there cannot exift long any equality between them in point of right and authority. Laftly, there fhould be little or no luxury ; for luxury muft either be the effect of wealth, or it muft make it neceffary ; it corrupts at once both rich and poor ; the one by means of the poffeffion of wealth, and the other by means of the want of it. Luxury makes a facrifice of

pa-

patriotifm to indolence and vanity; it robs a
ftate of its citizens by fubjecting them to each
other, and by fubjecting all to the influence of
public prejudice.

It is for this reafon that a certain celebrated
author hath laid down virtue as the firft principle of a republican government : for all thefe
circumftances cannot concur without the exiftence of public virtue. For want, however,
of making proper diftinctions, this great genius
hath been led into frequent miftakes, as well
as want of precifion ; not having obferved that,
the fovereign authority being every where the
fame, the fame principle muft take place in every
well conftituted ftate ; though it is true in a
greater or lefs degree, according to the form of
government.

To this it may be added, that no government
is fo fubject to civil wars and inteftine commotions as that of the democratical or popular
form; becaufe no other tends fo ftrongly and
fo conftantly to alter, nor requires fo much vi-
gilance and fortitude to preferve it from alteration. It is, indeed, in fuch a conftitution particularly that the citizen fhould always be arm-
ed

ed with force and conftancy, and fhould repeat every day, in the fincerity of his heart, the faying of the virtuous palatine *. *Malo periculfam libertatem quam quietum fervitium.*

Did there exift a nation of Gods, their government would doubtlefs be democratical; it is too perfect a form, however, for mankind.

CHAP. V.

Of an Ariftocra'y.

IN this form of government exift two moral perfons, very palpably diftinct, viz. the adminiftration and the fovereign; which of courfe poffefs two general wills, the one regarding the citizens univerfally; the other only the members of the adminiftration. Thus, although the government may regulate the interior police of the ftate as it pleafes, it cannot addrefs the people but in the name of the fovereign, that is to fay, the people themfelves; which is a circumftance never to be omitted. The primitive focieties of mankind were governed ariftocrati-

* The Palatine of Pofnania, father of the king of Poland, Duke of Lorra'n.

cally.

cally. The heads of families deliberated among themfelves concerning public affairs; the young people readily fubmitting to the authority of experience. Hence the names of *Priefts*, the *Fathers*, the *Senate*, &c. The favages of North America are governed in the fame manner to this day, and are extremely well governed.

But, in proportion as the inequality arifing from focial inftitutions prevailed over natural inequality, riches and power were preferred to age *, and the ariftocracy became elective. At length power, tranfmitted with property from father to fon, making whole families patrician, rendered the government hereditary, and boys of twenty became fenators.

Ariftocracy therefore is of three kinds; natural, elective and hereditary. The firft, is applicable only to the moft fimple ftate of fociety, while the laft is the worft of all kinds of government. The fecond is the beft; and is what is moft properly denominated an ariftocracy.

* It is evident that the term *optimates* among the ancients, did not mean the beft, but moft powerful.

Befide

Befide the advantage of the abovementioned
diftinction, this form hath alfo that of the
choice of its members: in a popular government all the citizens are born magiftrates; but
in this the number of the latter are very limited, and they become fuch only by election *;
a method by which their probity, their talents,
their experience, and all thofe other reafons
for preference in the public efteem, are an additional fecurity that the people fhall be wifely
governed.

Again, their public affemblies are attended
with more decorum; affairs of ftate are more
regularly difcuffed, and bufinefs executed with
greater order and expedition; while the credit
of the ftate is better fupported, in the eyes of
foreigners, by a felect number of venerable
fenators, than by a promifcuous or contemptible
mob.

* It is of great importance to regulate by law the
method of chufing magiftrates; for, in leaving this
to the prince, it is impoffible to avoid falling into an
hereditary ariftocracy, as happened to the republics
of Venice and Berne. Hence the firft has been long
fince diffolved, but the fecond hath been fupported
by the great prudence of the Senate. This is an exception, however, as dangerous as honourable.

In

In a word, that order would be undoubtedly the beſt and- moſt natural, according to
which the wiſe and experienced few direct the
multitude, were it certain that the few would
in their government conſult the intereſt of the
majority governed, and not their own.   It is ab-
ſurd to multiply the ſprings of action to no pur-
poſe, or to employ twenty thouſand men in
doing that, which an hundred properly ſelected
would effect much better.

With regard to the particular circumſtances
requiſite to this form of government ; the ſtate
ſhould not be ſo ſmall, nor the manners of the
people ſo ſimple or ſo virtuous as that the execution of the laws ſhould coincide with the
public Will, as in a well founded democracy.
On the other hand alſo, the ſtate ſhould not be
ſo extenſive that the governors, diſtributed up
and down its provinces, might be able to render
themſelves, each in his ſeparate department,
independant of the ſovereign.

But if an ariſtocracy requires fewer virtues
than a popular government ; there are yet ſome
which are peculiar to it ; ſuch as moderation in
the rich and content in the poor : an exact equality

lity of condition would in such a government be quite improper : nor was it observed even at Sparta.

If a certain degree however, of inequality in the fortunes of the people, be proper in such a government; the reason of it is, that in general the administration of public affairs, ought to be put into the hands of those persons who can best devote their time to such service; not, as Aristotle pretends, that the rich ought always to be preferred merely on account of their wealth. On the contrary, it is very necessary that an opposite choice should sometimes teach the people that there exist other motives of preference much more important than riches.

C H A P. VI.

On monarchy.

HITHERTO we have considered the prince as a moral and collective personage, formed by the force of the laws, and as the depository of the executive power of the state. At present, it is our business to consider this power, as lodged in the hands of a physical personage or real man; possessed of the right of

ex-

exerting it agreeable to the laws. Such a perfon is denominated a monarch or king.

In other adminiftrations it is common for a
collective body to reprefent an individual being ;
whereas in this an individual is, on the contrary, the reprefentative of a collective body ;
fo that the moral unity which conftitutes the
prince, is at the fame time a phyfical unity, in
which all the faculties which the law combines
in the former are combined naturally in the
latter.

Thus the will of the people and that of the
prince, together with the public force of the
ftate, and the particular force of the government, all depend on the fame principle of action :
all the fprings of the machine are in the fame
hand, are exerted to the fame end ; there are no
oppofite motions counteracting and deftroying
each other ; nor is it poffible to conceive any
fpecies of government in which the leaft effort
is productive of fo great a quantity of action.
Archimedes, fitting at his eafe on the fhore,
and moving about a large veffel on the ocean
at pleafure, reprefents to my imagination an able
monarch fitting in his cabinet, and governing
his diftant provinces, by keeping every thing in
                                        motion,

motion, while he himfelf feems immoveable.
But, if no other kind of government hath
fo much activity, there is none in which the
particular will of the individual is fo predomi-
nant. Every thing, it is true, proceeds toward
the fame end ; but this end is not that of public happinefs ; and hence the force of the adminiftration operates inceffantly to the prejudice of
the ftate.

Kings would be abfolute, and they are fometimes told that their beft way to become fo, is
to make themfelves beloved by the people. This
maxim is doubtlefs a very fine one, and even in
fome refpects true. But unhappily it is laughed
at in courts. That power which arifes from
the love of the people is without doubt the
greateft : but it is fo precarious and conditional,
that princes have never been fatisfied with it.
Even the beft kings are defirous of having it in
their power to do ill when they pleafe, without
lofing their prerogatives. It is to no purpofe
that a declaiming politician tells them that the
ftrength of the people being theirs, it is their
greateft intereft to have the people flourifhing,
numerous and refpectable : they know that this
is not true. Their perfonal and private intereft
is,

is, in the firſt place, that the people ſhould be
ſo weak and miſerable as to be incapable of making any reſiſtance to government.   I confeſs
indeed that, ſuppoſing the people to be held in
perfect ſubjection, it would be to the intereſt
of the prince that they ſhould be rich and
powerful, becauſe their ſtrength, being alſo
his, ſerves to make him reſpectable to his neighbours; but as this intereſt is only ſecondary
and ſubordinate, and that theſe ſuppoſitions are
incompatible, it is natural for princes to give
the preference always to that maxim which is
the moſt immediately uſeful.   This is what
Samuel hath repreſented very forcibly to the
Hebrews ; and Machiavel hath made evident to a
demonſtration.   In affecting to give inſtructions
to kings, he hath given the moſt ſtriking leſſons
to the people: His book entitled the Prince, is
particularly adapted to the ſervice of Republics.

We have already ſhewn from the general relations of things, that a monarchy is ſuitable only
to great ſtates, and we ſhall be more particularly
convinced of it, on a further examination.   The
more numerous the members of the public adminiſtration, the more is the relation beween
the prince and the ſubjects diminiſhed, and the
nearer

nearer it approaches to nothing, or that point of
equality which fubfifts in a democracy. This
relation increafes in proportion as the government
is contracted ; and arrives at its *maximum* when
the adminiftration is in the hands of a fingle
perfon. In this cafe, then, there is too great
a diftance between the prince and people, and
the ftate is void of connection. To fupply its
place, therefore, recourfe is had to the inter-
mediate ranks of people. Hence the feveral
orders of nobility. But nothing of this kind
is fuitable to a fmall ftate, to which thefe different ranks are very deftructive.

If the good government of a ftate be a matter of difficulty under any mode of adminiftration, it is more particularly fo in the hands of
a fingle perfon ; and every body knows the
confequences when a king reigns by fubftitutes.

Again, there is one effential and unavoidable
defect, which will ever render a monarchical government inferior to a republic ; and this is, that
in the latter, the public voice hardly ever raifes
unworthy perfons to high pofts in the adminiftration ; making choice only of men of knowlege and abilities, who difcharge their refpective

G   functions

functions with honour: whereas thofe who generally make their way to fuch pofts under a
monarchical government, are men of little minds
and mean talents, who owe their preferment to
the meritricious arts of flattery and intrigue. The
public are lefs apt to be deceived in their choice
than the prince; and a man of real merit is as rarely
to be found in the miniftry of a king, as a block-
head at the head of a republic. Thus, when
by any fortunate accident, a genius born for government, takes the lead in a monarchy, brought
to the verge of ruin by fuch petty rulers, the
world is amazed at the refources he difcovers,
and his adminiftration ftands as a fingular epoch
in the hiftory of his country.

To have a monarchical ftate well governed,
it is requifite that its magnitude or extent fhould
be proportioned to the abilities of the regent.
It is more eafy to conquer than to govern. By
means of a lever fufficiently long, it were poffible with a fingle finger to move the globe;
but to fupport it requires the fhoulders of an
Hercules. When a ftate may with any propriety be denominated great, the prince is almoft always too little. And when, on the contrary, it happens, which however is very feldom,

that

that the ſtate is too little for its regent, it muſt be ever ill-governed; becauſe the chief, actuated by the greatneſs of his own ideas, is apt to forget the intereſt of his people, and makes them no leſs unhappy from the abuſe of his ſuperfluous talents, than would another of a more limited capacity, for want of thoſe talents which ſhould be neceſſary. It is thence requi-ſite, that a kingdom ſhould, if I may ſo ſay, contract and dilate itſelf, on every ſucceſſion, according to the capacity of the reigning prince: whereas the abilities of a ſenate being more fixt, the ſtate, under a republican government, may be confined or extended to any determinate li-mits, and the adminiſtration be equally good. The moſt palpable inconvenience in the go-vernment of a ſole magiſtrate, is the default of that continued ſucceſſion, which, in the two other kinds, forms an uninterrupted connection in the ſtate. When one king dies, it is neceſſary to have another; but when kings are elective, ſuch elections form very turbulent and dange-rous intervals; and unleſs the citizens are poſ-ſeſſed of a diſintereſtedneſs and integrity, in-compatible with this mode of government, ve-nality and corruption will neceſſarily have an influence over them. It is very rare that he, to whom the ftate is fold, does not fell it again in his turn, and make the weak repay him the money extorted from him by the ftrong. Every one becomes, fooner or later, venal and corrupt, under fuch an adminiftration ; while even the tranquillity, which is enjoyed under the kings, is worfe than the diforder attending their *inter-regnum.*

To remedy thefe evils, crowns have been made hereditary, and an order of fucceffion hath been eftablifhed, which prevents any difputes on the death of kings : that is to fay, by fub-ftituting the inconvenience of regencies to that of elections, an apparent tranquillity is preferred to a wife adminiftration ; and it is thought bet-ter to run the rifk of having the throne fup-plied by children, monfters, and ideots, than to have any difpute about the choice of good kings. It is not confidered, that in expofing a ftate to the rifk of fuch an alternative, almoft every chance is againft it.

Almoft every thing confpires to deprive a youth, educated to the command over others, of the principles of reafon and juftice. Great pains, it is faid, are taken to teach young princes the art

of

of reigning; it does not appear however that they profit much by their education. It would be better to begin by teaching them fubjection. The greateſt monarchs that have been celebrated in hiſtory, are thoſe who were not educated to govern. This is a ſcience of which thoſe know the leaſt who have been taught the moſt, and is better acquired by ſtudying obedience than command. *Nam utilliſſimus idem ac breviſſimus bonarum malarumque rerum delectus, cogitare quid aut nolueris ſub alio principe aut volueris.*

A confequence of this want of coherence, is the inconſtancy of regal government, which is ſometimes purſued on one plan, and ſometimes on another, according to the character of the prince who governs, or of thoſe who hold the reins of adminiſtration for him ; fo that its conduct is as inconſiſtent as the object of its purſuit is wavering. It is this inconſtancy which keeps the ſtate ever fluctuating from maxim to maxim, and from project to project ; an uncertainty which does not take place in other kinds of government, where the prince is always the fame. Thus we fee, in general, that if there be more cunning in a court, there is more true

G 3   wiſdom

wifdom in a fenate ; and that republics accomplifh their ends, by means more conftant and
better purfued : while on the contrary, 'every
revolution in the miniftry of a court, produces
one in the ftate : it being the conftant maxim
with all minifters, and almoft with all kings,
to engage in meafures directly oppofite to thofe
of their immediate predeceffors. Again, it is
from this very incoherence that we may deduce
the folution of a fophifm very common with
regal politicians ; and this is not only the practice of comparing the civil government of fociety to the domeftic government of a family,
and the prince to the father of it, (an error
already expofed) but alfo that of liberally be-
ftowing on the reigning magiftrate all the virtues
he ftands in need of, and of fuppofing the
prince always fuch as he ought to be. With
the help of this fuppofition, indeed, the regal
government is evidently preferable to all others,
becaufe it is inconteftably the ftrongeft ; and nothing more is required to make it alfo the beft,
than that the will of the prince fhould be conformable to the general will of the people.

But if, according to Plato, the king by nature is fo very rare a perfonage, how feldom
may we fuppofe nature and fortune hath
concurred to crown him ? If a regal education
alfo

alſo neceſſarily corrupts thoſe who receive it, what hopes can we have from a race of men thus educated ? It is a wilful error, therefore, to confound a regal government in general with the government of a good king. But, to ſee what this ſpecies of government is in itſelf, it muſt be conſidered under the direction of weak and wicked princes : for ſuch they generally are when they come to the throne, or ſuch the throne will make them. Theſe difficulties have not eſcaped the notice of ſome writers, but they do not ſeem to have been much embarraſſed by them. The remedy, ſay they, is to obey without murmuring. God ſends us bad things in his wrath, and we ought, to bear with them as chaſtiſements from on high. This way of talk is certainly very edifying ; but I conceive it would come with greater propriety from the pulpit, than from the pen of a politician. What ſhould we ſay of a phyſician who might promiſe miracles, and whoſe whole art ſhould conſiſt in preaching up patience and reſignation ? It is obvious enough that we muſt bear with a bad government, when we live under it ; the queſtion is to find a good one.

CHAP.

CHAP. VII.

Of mixed Governments.

THERE is no such thing, properly speaking, as a simple government. Even a sole chief must have inferior magistrates, and a popular government a chief. Thus in the distribution of the executive power there is always a gradation from the greater number to the less, with this difference that sometimes the greater number depends on the less, and at others the less on the greater.

Sometimes indeed the distribution is equal, either when the constituent parts depend mutually on each other, as in the English government; or when the authority of each part is independent, though imperfect, as in Poland. This last form is a bad one, because there is no union in such a government, and the several parts of the state want a due connection.

It is a question much agitated by politicians; Which is best, a simple or mixt government? The same answer however might be given to it,

as

as I have before made to the like queſtion concerning the forms of government in general.

A ſimple government is the beſt in itſelf,
though for no other reaſon than that it is ſimple.
But when the executive power is not ſufficiently
dependent on the legiſlative, that is to ſay, when
there is a greater diſproportion between the
prince and the ſovereign, than between the people and the prince, this defect muſt be remedied
by dividing the government ; in which caſe all
its parts would have no leſs authority over the
ſubject, and yet their diviſion would render
them collectively leſs powerful to oppoſe their
ſovereign.

The ſame inconvenience is prevented alſo by
eſtabliſhing a number of inferior magiſtrates,
which tend to preſerve a ballance between the
two powers, and to maintain their reſpective
prerogatives. In this caſe, however, the government is not properly of a mixt kind ; it is
only moderated.

The like means may alſo be employed to remedy an oppoſite inconvenience, as when a government is too feeble, by erecting of proper
tribunals

tribunals to concentrate its force. This method is practised in all democracies. In the firft
cafe, the adminiftration is divided in order to
weaken it, and in the fecond to enforce it : For
a *maximum* both of ftrength and weaknefs, is
equally common to fimple governments, while
thofe of mixt forms always give a mean proportional to both.

C H A P. VIII.

*That every form of government is not equally
proper for every country.*

AS liberty is not the produce of all climates,
fo it is not alike attainable by all people.
The more one reflects on this principle, eftablifhed by Montefquieu, the more fenfible we
become of its truth. The more it is contefted,
the more we find it confirmed by new proofs.

Under every kind of government, the political perfonage, the public, confumes much,
but produces nothing. Whence then doth it
derive the fubftance confumed ? Evidently from
the labour of its members. It is from the fuperfluity of individuals that the neceffities of
the public are provided. Hence it follows
that

that a focial ftate cannot fubfift longer than the induftry of its members continues to produce fuch fuperfluity.

The quantity of this fuperfluity, however, is not the fame in all countries. It is in many very confiderable, in fome but moderate, in others null, and again in others negative. The proportion depends on the fertility of the climate, the fpecies of labour required in the cultivation of the foil, the nature of its produce, the ftrength of its inhabitants, the confumption neceffary to their fubfiftence, with many other fimilar circumftances.

On the other hand, all governments are not of the fame nature; fome devour much more than others, and their difference is founded on this principle, viz. that the farther public contributions are removed from their fource, the more burthenfome they grow. It is not by the quantity of the impofition that we are to eftimate the burthen of it, but by the time or fpace taken up in its returning back to the hands from which it is exacted. When this return is quick and eafy, it matters little whether fuch impofition be fmall or great; the people are

al-

always rich, and the finances in good condition. On the contrary, however low a people be taxed, if the money never returns, they are sure by constantly paying to be soon exhausted; such a state can never be rich, and the individuals of it must be always beggars.

It follows hence that the farther the people are removed from the seat of government, the more burthensome are their taxes: thus in a democracy their weight is least felt: in an aristocracy they fall more heavy; and in a monarchical state they have the greatest weight of all. Monarchy, therefore, is proper only for opulent nations; aristocracy for middling states; and a democracy for those which are mean and poor.

In fact, the more we reflect on this circumstance, the more plainly we perceive the difference in this respect between a monarchical and a free state. In the latter, all its force is exerted for the public utility; in the former, the public interest of the state and the private interest of the prince are reciprocally opposed; the one increasing by the decrease of the other.

In

In a word, inftead of governing fubjects in fuch a manner as to make them happy, defpotifm makes them miferable, in order to be able to govern them at all.

Thus may we trace in every climate thofe natural caufes, which point out that particular form of government which is beft adapted to it, as well as even the peculiar kind of people that fhould inhabit it. Barren and ungrateful foils, whofe produce will not pay for the labour of cultivation, would remain uncultivated and uninhabited, or, at beft, would be peopled only with favages. Thofe countries from which the inhabitants might draw the neceffaries of life, and no more, would be peopled by barbarians, among whom the eftablifhment of civil polity would be impoffible. Such places as might yield to their inhabitants a moderate fuperfluity, would be beft adapted to a free people ; while the country where fertile plains and plenteous vales more bounteoufly reward the labours of the cultivator, would beft fuit with a monarchical form of government, in order that the luxury of the prince might confume the fuperfluity' of the fubjects : for it is much better that this fuperfluity fhould be expended by government than diffipated by individuals. I am not infenfible that fome exceptions

7

ceptions might be made to what is here advanced; thefe very exceptions, however, ferve
to confirm the general rule, in that they are
fooner or later conftantly productive of revolutions, which reduce things to their natural
order.

We fhould always make a diftinction between
general laws, and thofe particular caufes which
may diverfify their effects. For, though the
fouthern climates fhould be actually filled with
republics, and the .northern with defpotic
monarchies, it would be neverthelefs true in
theory, that, fo far as climate is concerned, defpotifm agrees beft with an hot, barbarifm with
a cold, and good polity with a temperate re-
gion. I am aware farther that, even granting
the principle, the application of it may be dif-
puted. It may be faid, that fome cold countries are very fertile, while others more warm
and fouthern are very barren. This objection,
however, hath weight only with fuch as do not
examine the matter in every point of view. It
is requifite to take into confideration, as I before obferved, the labour of the people, their
ftrength, their confumption, with every other
circumftance that affects the point in queftion.

Let

Let us suppose two countries of equal extent, the proportion of whose product should be as five to ten. It is plain that, if the inhabitants of the first consume four, and of the latter nine, the superfluity of the one would be ¹, and that of the other ¹⁄₉. Their different superfluities being also in an inverse ratio to that of their produce, the territory whose produce should amount only to five, would have near double the superfluity of that which should amount to ten.

But the argument does not rest upon a double produce ; nay I doubt whether any person will place the actual fertility of cold countries in general, in a bare equality with that of warmer climates. We will suppose them, however, to be in this respect simply equal ; setting England, for instance, on a balance with Sicily, and Poland with Egypt. Still farther to the South we have Africa and the Indies, and to the North hardly any thing. But to effect this equality in the produce, what a difference in the labour of cultivation ! In Sicily they have nothing more to do than barely turn up the earth : in England agriculture is extremely toilsome and laborious. . Now, where a greater number of

hands

hands is required to raife the fame produce, the fuperfluity muft neceffarily be lefs.

Add to this, that the fame number of people confume much lefs in a warm country than in a cold one.   An hot climate requires men to be temperate, if they would preferve their health. Of this the Europeans are made fenfible, by feeing thofe who do not alter their manner of living in hot countries, daily carried off by dyfenteries and indigeftion.   Chardin reprefents us, as beafts of prey, as mere wolves in comparifon of the Afiatics; and thinks thofe writers miftaken, who have attributed the temperance of the Perfians, to the uncultivated ftate of their country.   His opinion is that their country was fo little cultivated, becaufe the inhabitants required fo little for their fubfiftence.   If their frugality were merely the effect of the barrennefs of their country, he obferves, it would be only the poorer fort of them that fhould eat little; whereas their abftinence is general.   Again, they would in fuch cafe be more or lefs abftemious in different provinces, as thofe provinces differed in degrees of fterility; whereas their fobriety is general, and prevails equally throughout the kingdom.   He tells
us,

us, alſo, that the Perſians boaſt much of their
manner of living ; pretending their complexions
only to be a ſufficient indication, of its being
preferable to that of the Chriſtians. At the
ſame time, he admits that their complexions
are very fine and ſmooth ; that their ſkin is of
a ſoft texture, and poliſhed appearance ;
while, on the other hand, the complexion of
the Armenians, their ſubjects, who live after
the European manner, is rough and pimply,
and their bodies groſs and unwieldy.

The nearer we approach to the line, it is
certain, the more abſtemious we find the people. They hardly ever eat meat ; rice and maize
are their ordinary food. There are millions of
people in the Indies, whoſe ſubſiſtence does not
amount to the value of a penny a day. We
ſee even in Europe, a very ſenſible difference,
in this reſpect, between the inhabitants of the
North and South. A Spaniard will ſubſiſt a
whole week, on what a German would eat up
at a ſingle meal. In countries where the people are voracious, even luxury hath a tendency
to conſumption. Thus in England it diſplays
itſelf in the number of diſhes and quantity of
ſolid meat on the table ; while in Italy, a re-
paſt

paſt is furniſhed out with ſweetmeats and
flowers.

The luxury of dreſs preſents us, alſo, with
ſimilar differences.   In climates, where the
change of the weather is ſudden and violent,
the people wear better and plainer clothes ;
while in thoſe where the inhabitants dreſs only
for ornament, brilliancy is more conſulted than
uſe ; even clothes themſelves are an article of
luxury.   Thus at Naples, you will daily ſee
gentlemen walking about in laced clothes without ſtockings. It is the ſame with regard to
buildings : magnificence only is conſulted, where
nothing is to be feared from the inclemencies of
the weather.   At Paris and London people are
deſirous of warm and commodious apartments.
At Madrid, they have ſuperb ſaloons, but no
ſaſhes nor caſements ; and their beds lie open
to the rats that harbour in the roof.

The aliment is alſo more ſubſtantial and nou-
riſhing in hot countries than in cold ; this is a third
difference that cannot fail to have an influence
over the ſecond. Wherefore is it that the Italians
eat ſuch a quantity of vegetables ? Becauſe they
are good, and of an excellent ſavour. In France,
                                                    where

where they are themselves nourished chiefly by water, they are less nutritive, and are held of little consequence. They occupy nevertheless as much ground, and cost as much pains to cultivate them. It hath been experimentally proved that the corn of Barbary, in other respects inferior to that of France, gives a greater quantity of meal, and that the French corn yields still more than that of the North. Hence it may be inferred that a similar gradation is carried on in the same direction from the line to the pole. Now is it not an evident disadvantage to have, in an equal produce, a less quantity of aliment?

To all these different considerations, I may add another, which arises from, and serves to confirm them; this is, that hot countries require fewer inhabitants than the cold, and yet afford subsistence for more; a circumstance that causes a two-fold superfluity, always to the advantage of despotism. The more the same number of people are distributed over the face of a large territory, the more difficult becomes a revolt; as they cannot meet together so readily or secretly, and it is always easy for the government to cut off their associations, and ruin their projects.

jects. On the other hand, the more a numerous people are collected together, the lefs can
the government affume over the fovereign ; the
chiefs of a faction may deliberate as fecurely
at their meetings, as the prince in his council ;
and the mob are as readily affembled in the
public fquares as the troops in their quarters.
It is the advantage of a tyrannical government,
therefore, to act at great diftances ; its force
increafing with the diftance like that of a lever *,
by the affiftance of a proper center. That of
the people, on the contrary, acts only by being
concentrated ; it evaporates and lofes itfelf when
dilated, even as gunpowder fcattered on the
ground, takes fire, particle by particle, and is
productive of no effect. Countries thinly in-

---

* This doth not contradict what is advanced in,
Chap. ix. Book II. concerning the inconvenience of
great ftates ; the matter in queftion there being the
authority of the government over its members, and
here of its influence over the fubjects. Its members,
fcattered about in different places, ferve as points
of fupport to enable it to act at a diftance on the people ; but it hath no fuch props to affift its action
on its members themfelves. Thus in one cafe the
length of the lever is the caufe of its ftrength, and
in the other of its weaknefs.

habited

habited are the moſt proper places for tyrants ;
wild beaſts reign only in deſarts.

C H A P. IX.

Of the marks of a good Government.

WHEN it is aſked, therefore, in general
terms, what is the beſt form of government ? the queſtion is as indeterminate as
unanſwerable : or rather it may be reaſonably
anſwered as many different ways as there are
poſſible combinations of the abſolute and relative circumſtances of a people.

But if it be aſked, by what ſigns it may be
known whether any given people are well or ill
governed ? This is quite another thing, and
the queſtion, as to the faɛt, is to be reſolved.

This queſtion, however, is never actually reſolved, becauſe every one is for doing it after
his own manner. The ſubject cries up the public
tranquillity, the citizen the liberty of individuals ;
the one prefers the ſecurity of property, the
other that of his perſon ; the one maintains
the beſt government to be the moſt ſevere, the
other affirms that to be beſt which is moſt agreeable ;

able; the latter is for punishing crimes, the
former for preventing them: the one thinks it
a fine thing to be dreaded by his neighbours;
the other thinks it better to be unknown to
them; the one is satisfied if money does but
circulate, the other requires the people should
have bread. Were they even agreed also on
these and other similar points, they would not
be much nearer the end of the dispute. Moral
quantities are deficient in point of precision;
so that, were men agreed on the sign, they
would still differ about its estimation.

For my part, I am astonished that a sign so
very simple should be mistaken, or that any
should be so disingenuous as not to acknowlege
it. What is the end of political society? doubt-
less the preservation and prosperity of its
members. And what is the most certain sign
or proof of these? Certainly it is their number
and population. Let us not look elsewhere,
then, for this disputed proof; since it is plain,
that government must be the best, under which
the citizens increase and multiply most, sup-
posing all other circumstances equal, and no
foreigners naturalized or colonies introduced,
to cause such increase: and that, on the
contrary

contrary, that government muſt be the worſt, under which, *cætris paribus*, the number of people ſhould diminiſh. This being admitted, the deciſion of the queſtion becomes an affair of calculation *, and as ſuch I give it up to the arithmeticians.

CHAP.

* It is on the ſame principle that we ought to judge of the ſeveral perioes of time that deſerve the preference, in being diſtinguiſhed for the proſperity of mankind. We have in general too much admired thoſe, in which literature and the fine arts have flouriſhed, without penetrating into the ſecret cauſe of their cultivation, or duly conſidering their fatal effects; *idque aſud inperites hum nitas vicabatur, cum pars ſervitutis effet.* Shall we never be able to ſee through the maxims laid down in books, the intereſted motives of their authors ?—No, let writers ſay what they will, whenever the inhabitants of a country decreaſe, it is not true that all things go well, whatever be its external proſperity and ſplendour : A poet poſſeſſed of an hundred thouſand livres a year, does not neceſſarily make the age he lives in the beſt of all others. We ſhould not ſo much regard the apparent repoſe of the w rld, and the tranquillity of its chiefs, as the well being of whole nations, and particularly of the moſt populous ſtates. A ſtorm of hail may lay waſte ſome few provinces, but it ſeldom cauſes a famine. Temporary tumults and
civil

CHAP. X.

Of the abuse of government, and its tendency to degenerate.

AS the particular will of the prince acts
constantly against the general will of the
people, the government necessarily makes a continual effort against the sovereignty. The greater
this effort is, the more is the constitution altered ; and as in this case there is no other di-
stinct Will to keep that of the prince in equilibrio, it must sooner or later infallibly happen
that

civil wars may give much disturbance to rulers ; but
they do not constitute the real misfortunes of a people, who may even enjoy some respite, while they
are disputing who shall play the tyrant over them.
It is from their permanent situation that their real
prosperity or calamity must arise : when all submit
tamely to the yoke, then it is that all are perishing ;
then it is that their chiefs, destroying them at their ease,
ubi solitudinem faciunt pacem appellant. When the in-
trigues of the nobility agitated the kingdom of France,
and the coadjutor of Paris carried a poignard in his
pocket to parliament ; all this did not hinder the bulk
of the French nation from growing numerous and
en-

that the prince will opprefs the fovereign, and break the focial compact. This is an inherent and unavoidable defect, which from the very birth of the political body, inceffantly tends to its diffolution, even as old age and death tend to the diffolution of the natural body.

There are two general methods according to which a government degenerates; viz. when it contracts itfelf, or when the ftate is diffolved. The government contracts itfelf, when its members are reduced from a great number to a few; that is to fay, from a democracy to an aristocracy, and from an ariftocracy to a royalty.

enjoying themfelves in happinefs and eafe. Ancient Greece flourifhed in the midft of the moft cruel wars: human blood was fpilt in torrents, and yet the country fwarmed with inhabitants. It appears, fays Machiavel, that, in the midft of murders, profcriptions and civil wars, our republic became only the more powerful, the virtue of the citizens, their manners, their independence had a greater effect to ftrengthen it, than all its diffentions had to weaken it. A little agitation gives vigour to the mind, and liberty, not peace, is the real fource of the profperity of our fpecies.

H

This

This is its natural tendency *.   Should it make
a retrogreſſive change, by having the number
of

* The ſlow formation and progreſs of the republic of Venice, preſent a notable example of this
ſucceſſion ; and it is very ſurpriſing that in the ſpace
of 1200 years the Venetians ſhould be got no farther
than to the ſecond term, which began in the year
1198. With regard to the ancient dukes, with
which their conſtitution is reproached, it is certain,
whatever ſome writers may ſay, that they were not
ſovereigns.

The Roman republic will, doubtleſs, be made an
objection, as having taken a contrary route, in its
progreſs from monarchy to ariſtocracy, and from
ariſtocracy to democracy. I am, however, far from
thinking this was the real caſe.

The firſt eſtabliſhment of Romulus was a mixt
government, which degenerated preſently into deſpotiſm. From very particular cauſes the ſtate periſh-
ed before its time, as a new born infant, before it
attained the age of manhood. The expulſion of the
Tarquins, was the true era of the riſe of that republic ; although it did not aſſume at firſt a determinate
form ; becauſe the work was but half done, in not
having aboliſhed the order of patricians. For hence,
an hereditary ariſtocracy, the worſt of all admini-
ſtrations,

of its members increafed, it might be faid to relax or dilate itfelf; but this inverfe progrefs is impoffible.

In faƈt, a government never changes its form, except its fpring of aƈtion be too much worn to fupport its own. Now, if it relaxes ftill more, by being extended, its force becomes abfolutely nothing,

ftrations, aƈting in oppofition to the democracy, the form of government remained indeterminate; not being fixed, as Machiavel obferves, till the eftablifh-ment of the tribunes; when, and not before, it was a real government under the form of a true democra-cy. In faƈt, the people were then not only fovereign, but alfo magiftrate and judge; the fenate being a tri-bunal of an inferior order, formed to temper and colleƈt the government; while even the confuls them-felves although patricians, firft magiftrates, and as ge-nerals abfolute in the field, yet at Rome they were only prefidents of the affemblies of the people.

From this time it is evident the government fol-lowed its natural byafs, and tended ftrongly toward ariftocracy. The patrician order dying away of it-felf, the ariftocracy fubfifted no longer in the members of that body, as at Venice and Genoa, but in the body of the fenate compofed of Patricians and Ple-beians, and even in the body of tribunes when they

began

nothing, and is ſtill leſs capable of ſupporting itſelf. It is neceſſary therefore to wind up and renew ſuch ſpring in proportion as it gives way ; otherwiſe the ſtate it is intended to ſupport, muſt neceſſarily fall.

The diſſolution of the ſtate indeed may happen two ways. Firſt, when the prince does not govern according to law; but arrogates the ſovereign power to himſelf: in which caſe he effects a remarkable change, whereby not the government, but the ſtate itſelf is contracted. What I mean to ſay is, that the great ſtate is thence diſſolved, and that he forms another within it, compoſed only of the members of the government, who are only the maſters and tyrants over the reſt of the people. So

began to uſurp an active power. For words make no alteration in things. When the people have chiefs who govern in their ſtead, whatever denomination be given to thoſe chiefs, the government is always an ariſtocracy. From the abuſe of the ariſtocratical form, aroſe the civil wars and the triumvirate. Sylla, Julius Cæſar and Auguſtus indeed became real monarchs, and at length under the deſpotiſm of Tiberius the ſtate was finally diſſolved. The Roman hiſtory, therefore, doth not tend to diſprove my principle, but to confirm it.

that

that when the government ufurps the fovereignty, at that inftant the focial compact is broken,
and the individuals, who were citizens before,
are reftored to the rights of natural liberty,
and are compelled, not legally obliged, to
obedience.

It is the fame thing, when the members of
government affume feparately the power they
are entitled to exercife only collectively; which
is no lefs an infringement of the laws, and is
productive of ftill worfe confequences. For,
in this cafe, there may be faid to be as many
princes as magiftrates; while the ftate no lefs
divided than the government, is totally diffolved
or changes its form.

When the ftate is diffolved, the abufe of
government, of whatever nature it be, takes
the common name of anarchy. To diftinguifh
more nicely, *democracy* is faid to degenerate into
ochlocracy; *ariftocracy* into *oligarchy*; and I
may add *monarchy* into *tyranny*: but this laft
term is equivocal, and requires fome explanation. In the vulgar fenfe of the word, a tyrant
is a king who governs by force and without
regard to juftice or the laws. In the more precife and determinate fenfe, it means any indi-

H 3 vidual

vidual who affumes the royal authority, without having a right to it.   In this latter fenfe the
Greeks underftood the word tyrant ; and give
it indifcriminately both to good and bad princes
whofe authority was not legal *.   Thus, *tyrant* and *ufurper* are two words perfectly fy-
nonimous.

To give different names, however, to different things, I call the ufurpation of regal authority, *tyranny*, and that of fovereign power
defpotifm.   The tyrant is he, who takes
upon himfelf, contrary to law, to govern according to law ; and the defpotic chief, one
who places himfelf above the laws themfelves.
Thus a tyrant cannot be defpotic, though a
defpotic prince muft always be a tyrant.

* *Omnes enim et habentur et dicuntur tyranni qui potestate utuntur perpetuâ, in eâ civitate quæ libertate ufa eft.* CORN. NEPOS. IN MILTIADE.   It is true
that Ariftotle makes a diftinction between the tyrant
and king, in that the one governs for his own good,
and the other for the good of his fubjects : but, befides that all the Greek writers ufe the word tyrant
in a different fenfe, as appears particularly by the
Hieron of Zenophon, it would follow from Ariftotle's
diftinction that no king ever exifted on the face of
the earth.

C H A P.

CHAP. XI.

Of the diffolution of the body politic.

SUCH is the natural and unavoidable tendency of even the beft conftituted governments. If Rome and Sparta perifhed, what ftate can hope to laft for ever? In our endeavours to form a durable eftablifhment, we muft not think, therefore, to make it eternal. If we would hope to fucceed, we muft not attempt impoffibilities, nor flatter ourfelves to give that permanency to human inftitutions, which is incompatible with their nature.

The body politic, as well as the phyfical, begins to die at its birth, and bears in itfelf the caufes of its deftruction. Both, however, may poffefs a conftitution more or lefs robuft, and adapted to different periods of duration. The conftitution of man is the work of nature; that of the ftate, is the work of art. It doth not depend on men to prolong their lives, but it depends on them to prolong that of the ftate as much as poffible, by giving it a conftitution the beft adapted to longevity. The moft perfect conftitution, it is true, will have an end;

H 4

but

but ſtill ſo much later than others, if no un-
foreſeen accident bring it to an untimely diſſolution.

The principle of political life, lies in the
ſovereign authority. The legiſlative power is
the heart of the ſtate; the executive power is
the brain, which puts every part in motion.
The brain may be rendered uſeleſs by the palſy,
and yet the individual ſurvive. A man may be·
come an inſenſible driveller and yet live: but
as ſoon as the heart ceaſes to beat, the animal
is dead.

The ſtate doth not ſubſiſt by virtue of the
laws, but by the legiſlative power. The ſta-
tutes of yeſterday are not in themſelves neceſſarily binding to day, but the tacit confirmation
of them is preſumed from the ſilence of the
legiſlature; the ſovereign being ſuppoſed in·
ceſſantly to confirm the laws not actually repealed. Whatever is once declared to be the
will of the ſovereign, continues always ſo, unleſs it be abrogated.

Wherefore, then, is there ſo much reſpect
paid to ancient laws? Even for this reaſon. It
is rational to ſuppoſe, that nothing but the
ex-

excellence of the ancient laws, could preserve them fo long in being; for that, if the fovereign had not found them always falutary and ufeful, they would have been repealed.

Hence we fee that the laws, inftead of lofing their force, acquire additional authority by time, in every well formed ftate; the prepoffeffion of their antiquity renders them every day more venerable; whereas, in every country where the laws grow obfolete and lofe their force as they grow old, this alone is a proof that the legiflative power itfelf is decayed, and the ftate extinct.

C H A P. XII.

By what means the fovereign authority is maintained.

THE fovereign, having no other force than the legiflative power, acts only by the laws; while the laws being only the authentic acts of the general will, the fovereign cannot act unlefs the people are affembled. The people affemble! you will fay. What a chimera?—It is indeed chimerical at prefent; though it was not reckoned fo two thou-

fand

fand years ago. Are mankind changed in their nature fince that time?

The bounds of poffibility in moral affairs are lefs confined than we are apt to imagine: It is our foibles, our vices, our prejudices that contract them. Mean fouls give no credit to the fentiments of heroic minds; while flaves affect to turn the notion of liberty, into ridicule.

By what hath been done, however, we may judge of what may be done again. I fhall not fpeak of the petty republics of ancient Greece; but the Roman republic was, undoubtedly, a great ftate, and the city of Rome a great city. By the laft regifter of the citizens of Rome, their number amounted to four hundred thoufand perfons capable of bearing arms; and the laft regifter of the Empire amounted to more than four millions of citizens, without reckoning fubjects, women, children or flaves.

How very difficult, you will fay, muft it have been, to affemble frequently the people of that capital and its environs? And yet hardly a week paffed in which the Roman people were not affembled, and on fome occafions feveral times a week.

I

a week. This numerous body indeed not only exercifed the functions of fovereignty, but alfo in fome cafes thofe of government. They fometimes deliberated on ftate affairs, and at others decided in judicial caufes; the whole people being publicly affembled almoft as frequently in the capacity of magiftrates as citizens.

By recurring to the primitive ftate of nations, we fhall find that moft of the ancient governments, even the monarchical, as that of the Macedon and others, had the like popular affemblies. Be this, however, as it may, the fact being once inconteftibly proved, obviates all difficulties; for, to deduce the poffibility of a thing from its having actually happened, will admit of no objection.

H 6   C H A P.

C H A P. XIII.

The subject continued.

IT is not enough, however, that the people once assembled should fix the constitution of the state, by giving their sanction to a certain code or system of laws : it is not enough that they should establish a perpetual government, or provide once for all by the election of ma-giftrates. Besides the extraordinary assemblies, which unforeseen accidents may require, it is necessary they should have certain fixed and pe-riodical meetings, which nothing might abolish or prorogue: so that the people should, on a certain day, be legally summoned by law, with-out any expres statute being required for their formal convocation.

But, excepting these regular assemblies, ren-dered legal by the date, all others, unless con-voked by the proper magistrate previously ap-pointed to that end, agreeable to prescribed forms, should be held illegal, and all their de-terminations declared null and void; because the very manner of the people's assembling should be determined by law.

As

As to the frequency of legal affemblies, it depends on fo many different confiderations, that it is impoffible to lay down any precife rules on this head. It can only be faid in general that the more powerful the government, the more often ought the fovereignty to difplay itfelf.

All this, it may be faid, is very well for a fingle town or city; but what muft be done in a ftate comprehending feveral cities? Muft the fovereign authority be diftributed, or ought it to centre in one, to the total fubjection of the reft?

I anfwer, neither one nor the other. In the firft place, the fovereign authority is fimple and uniform, fo that it cannot be divided without deftroying it. In the next place, one city cannot be legally fubject to another, any more than one nation to another; becaufe the effence of the body politic confifts in the union of obedience and liberty, and in the terms *fubject* and *fovereign* being thofe identical correlatives, the ideas of which are united in the fingle term *citizen.*

I anfwer

I anfwer farther, that it is fundamentally wrong, to unite feveral towns to form one city; and that fuch union being made, the natural inconveniences of it muft enfue. The abufes peculiar to great ftates muft not be made ob- jections to the fyftem of one, who maintains the exclufive propriety of little ones. But how, it will be faid, can little ftates be made powerful enough to refift the great?—Even as the cities of ancient Greece were able to refift the arms of a powerful monarch; and, as in more modern times, Switzerland and Holland, have refifted the power of the houfe of Auftria.

In cafes, alfo, where the ftate cannot be re- duced within proper bounds, there remains one refource; and this is by not permitting the ex- iftence of a capital, but removing the feat of go- vernment from one town to another, and affemb- ling the ftates of the country in each alternately.

People a country equally in every part; dif- fufe the fame privileges and advantages through- out; and the ftate will become at once the ftrongeft and the beft governed. Remember that the walls of cities are founded on the ruins of the villages, and that the fplendid palaces

in

in town are raifed at the expence of miferable cottages in the country.

C H A P. XIV.

Subject continued.

NO fooner are the people legally affembled, in a fovereign body, than the jurifdiction of government ceafes, the executive power of the ftate is fufpended, and the perfon of the meaneft citizen becomes as facred and inviolable as the greateft magiftrate; becaufe when the body reprefented appears, it is not requifite that the reprefentatives of it fhould exift. Moft of the tumults which happened in the *Comitia* at Rome, were owing to the general ignorance or neglect of this rule. On thofe occafions, the confuls were only prefidents of the affembly of the people, the tribunes merely orators *, and the fenate abfolutely nothing.

Thefe intervals of fufpenfion, when the prince acknowleges, or at leaft ought to ac-

* Nearly in the fenfe given to thofe who fpeak on any queftion in the parliament of England. The refemblance of their employments fet the confuls and tribunes together by the ears; even when their jurifdiction was fufpended.

knowlege

knowlege an actual superior, have been always formidable, while such formidable assemblies, the security of the body politic and the restraint of government, have been held in honour by the chiefs : so that they never have been sparing of pains, in raising objections and difficulties, or of making fair promises in order to disgust the citizens with such meetings.   When the latter, therefore, have been avaritious, mean, or cowardly, preferring their case to liberty, they have not been able to withstand long the repeated efforts of government : and thus it is that, this encroaching power incessantly augmenting, the sovereignty becomes totally extinct, and thus most cities come to an untimely end.

Sometimes, however, there is introduced between sovereign authority and arbitrary government, a mean term of power, of which it is necessary to treat.

CHAP.

CHAP. XV.

Of deputies or representatives.

WHEN the fervice of the public ceafes to be the principal concern of the citizens, and they had rather difcharge it by their purfes than their perfons, the state is already far advanced toward ruin. When they fhould march out to fight, they pay troops to fight for them, and ftay at home. When they fhould go to council, they fend deputies, and ftay at home. Thus, in confequence of their indolence and wealth, they in the end employ foldiers to enflave their country, and reprefentatives to betray it.

It is the buftle of commerce and the arts; it is the fordid love of gain, of luxury and eafe, that thus convert perfonal into pecuniary fervices. Men readily give up one part of their profit, to increafe the reft unmolefted. But fupply an adminiftration with money, and they will prefently fupply you with chains. The very term of *taxes* is flavifh, and unknown in a free city. In a ftate truly free, the citizens difcharge their duty to the public with their

own

own hands, and not by money. So far from
paying for being exempted from such duty,
they would pay to be permitted to difcharge it
themfelves. I am very far from adopting received opinions, and think the fervices exacted
by force a lefs infringement of liberty than
taxes.

The better the conftitution of a ftate, the
greater influence have public affairs over private,
in the minds of the citizens: They will have,
alfo, much fewer private affairs to concern
them ; becaufe the fum total of their common
happinefs, furnifhing a more confiderable portion to each individual, there remains the lefs
for each to feek from his own private concerns.
In a city well governed, every one is ready to
fly to its public affemblies ; under a bad government they are carelefs about going thither at
all; becaufe no one interefts himfelf in what
is doing there ; it is known that the general
will does not influence them, and hence at
length domeftic concerns engage all their attention.   Good laws tend to the making better,
while bad ones are introductory of Worfe.   No
fooner doth a citizen fay, what are ftate-affairs
to me ? than the ftate may be given up for
loft.

It.

It is this want of public fpirit, the influence of private intereft, the extent of ftates, conquefts and abufes in government, that have given rife to the method of affembling the people by deputies and reprefentatives. The affembly of thefe reprefentatives is called in fome countries, the third eftate of the nation; fo that the particular interefts of the two orders are placed in the firft and fecond rank, and the public intereft only in the third.

The fovereignty, however, cannot be reprefented, and that for the fame reafon that it cannot be alienated. It confifts effentially of the general will, and the will cannot be reprefented : it is either identically the fame, or fome other ; there can be no mean term in the cafe. The deputies of the people, therefore, neither are nor can be their reprefentatives ; they are only mere commiffioners, and can conclude definitively on nothing. Every law that is not confirmed by the people in perfon is null and void ; it is not in fact a law. The Englifh imagine they are a free people ; they are however miftaken : they are fuch only during the election of members of parliament. When thefe are chofen, they become flaves again ; and indeed they make fo bad a ufe of the few

tran-

tranfitory moments of liberty, that they richly
deferve to lofe it.

The notion of reprefentatives is modern; de-
fcending to us from the feudal fyftem, tnat moſt
iniquitous and abfurd form of government, by
which human nature was fo fhamefully degraded.
In the ancient republics, and even monarchies,
the people had no reprefentatives; they were
ftrangers to the term. It is even very fingular
that, at Rome, where the Tribunes were fo
much revered, it was never imagined they
could ufurp the functions of the people ; and as
ftrange that they never once attempted it. One
may judge, however, of the embarraſſment
fometimes caufed by the multitude, by what
happened in the time of the Gracchi, when
part of the citizens gave their votes from their
houfe-tops.

Where men value their liberty and privileges
above every thing, inconveniences and difficulties are nothing. Among this wife people things
were held in a proper eftimation ; they permitted the Lictors to do what they would
not fuffer the Tribunes to attempt ; they were not
afraid

afraid the Lictors would ever think of repre-
fenting them.

To explain, neverthelefs, in what manner
thefe Tribunes did fometimes reprefent them,
it will be fufficient to conceive how government reprefents the fovereign. The law being
only a declaration of the general will, it is clear
that the people cannot be reprefented in the legiflative power ; but they may, and ought to be, in
the executive ; which is only the application of
power to law. And this makes it evident that,
if we examine things to the bottom, we fhall
find very few nations that have any laws. But,
be this as it may, it is certain that the Tribunes, having no part of the executive power,
could not reprefent the Roman people, by virtue of their office, but only in ufurping thofe
of the fenate.

Among the Greeks, whatever the people had
to do, they did it in perfon ; they were perpetually affembled in public. They inhabited
a mild climate, were free from avarice, their
flaves managed their domeftic bufinefs, and
their great concern was liberty. As you do not
poffefs the fame advantages, how can you expect

pect to preserve the same privileges ? Your climate being more severe, creates more wants * ;
for six months in the year your public squares
are too wet or cold to be frequented ; your
hoarse tongues cannot make themselves heard
in the open air ; you apply yourselves more to
gain than to liberty, and are less afraid of slavery
than poverty.

On this occasion, it will probably be asked
me, if liberty cannot support itself without the
assistance of slavery ? Perhaps not. At least
the two extremes approach very near. Whatever does not exist in nature, must have its
conveniences, and civil society still more than
any thing else. There are some circumstances
so critically unhappy that men cannot preserve
their own liberty but at the expence of the liberty of others ; and in which a citizen cannot
be perfectly free without aggravating the sub-
jection of his slaves. Such was the situation
of Sparta. As for you, ye moderns, you have
no slaves, but are slaves yourselves, and purchase

To adopt in cold countries the luxury and ef-
feminacy of the East, is to appear desirous of slavery, without having the same excuse for submitting
to it.

their

their liberty by your own. You may if you
pleafe boaft of this preference; for my part,
I find more meannefs in it than humanity.

I do not intend, however, by this to inculcate
that we fhould have flaves, or that it is equitable to reduce men to a ftate of flavery; having already proved the contrary. I am here
only giving the reafons why certain modern nations who imagine themfelves free, employ reprefentatives, and why the ancients did not.
But let this be as it will, I affirm that when
once a people make choice of reprefentatives,
they are no longer free.

Every thing duly confidered, I do not fee a
poffibility of the fovereign maintaining its rights,
and the exercife of its prerogatives, for the
future among us, unlefs the ftate be indeed very
fmall. But if it be fo very fmall, will it not
be liable to lofe its independency? No. I
will make it hereafter appear in what manner
the exterior power of a great people may be
united with the policy and good order of a little
one.

CHA

CHAP. XVI.

That the inftitution of government is not a compact.

THE legiflative power being once well eftablifhed, we proceed to fettle the executive power in the fame manner: for the latter which operates only by particular acts, being effentially different from the other, is naturally divided from it. If it were poffible for the fovereign, confidered as fuch, to poffefs the executive power, the matter of right and fact would be fo confounded, that we fhould no longer be able to diftinguifh what is law and what is not; the body politic alfo being thus unnaturally fituated, would foon become a prey to that violence, which it was originally inftituted to correct.

The citizens being, by virtue of the focial compact, all equal, that which all may perform, all may prefcribe, whereas none can have a right to require another to do what he does not himfelf. Now it is properly this right, indifpenfibly neceffary to animate and put the body politic in motion, with which the fovereign invefts

vefts the prince in the inftitution of government.

It has been pretended by fome that the act forming this inftitution, was a contract between the people and the chiefs of which they made choice: a contract in which the two parties ftipulated the conditions on which the one obliged themfelves to command, and the other to obey. I am perfuaded every one will agree with me that this was a very ftrange mode of contract. But let us fee whether this opinion is in itfelf well founded.

In the firft place the fupreme authority can no more modify or alter its form than it can alienate itfelf; to limit or reftrain, would be to deftroy it. It is abfurd and contradictory to fay the fovereign made choice of a fuperior: to oblige itfelf to obey a mafter, is to diffolve its own conftitution, and reftore its members to their natural liberty.

Again, it is plain that fuch a fuppofed contract between the people in general and certain particular perfons would be a particular act; whence it follows that it would not be a law

nor

nor an act of sovereignty, and of consequence
would be illegal.

It is farther evident, that the contracting
parties would remain, respecting each other,
simply under the laws of nature, without any
security for the performance of their reciprocal
engagements, a circumstance totally repugnant
to a state of civil society.   The party only who
might have the power, could enforce the execution of the terms; so that we might as well give
the name of a contract, to the act of a man
who should say to another, " I give you my
whole property, on condition that you will re-
store me just as much of it as you please."

There is but one compact in a state, and that
is the act of association, which alone is exclusive of every other; as it is impossible to
imagine any subsequent public contract which
would not be a violation of the original.

C H A P.

CHAP. XVII.

Of the inflitution of government.

WHAT notion, then, are we ˏto form of the act, by which government is inftituted ? In anfwer to this queftion, I fhall firft remark that this act is complicated, or compofed of two others, viz the eftablifhment of the law and the execution of it.

ʹBy the firft, the fovereign enacts that a government fhall be eftablifhed in fuch or fuch a form ; and it is clear, this being a general act, that it is a law.

By the fecond, the people name the chiefs who are to be charged with the adminiftration of the government fo eftablifhed. Now this nomination, being a particular act, is not a fecond law, but only a confequence of the firft, and in reality an act of government.

The difficulty lies in being able to comprehend how an act of government can take place before the government exifted, and how the

I 2 people,

people, who muſt be always either ſovereign or
ſubjects, become prince or magiſtrate, in certain circumſtances.

We have here made a diſcovery of one of
theſe aſtoniſhing properties of the body politic,
by which it reconciles operations apparently
contradictory to each other ; this act being effected by a ſudden converſion of the ſovereignty
into a democracy : ſo that, without any ſenſible
change, and only by means of a new relation of
all to all, the citizens, becoming magiſtrates,
paſs from general acts to particular ones, and
from enacting laws to the execution of them.

This change of relation is not a matter of
mere ſpeculation, unexemplified in practice :
it takes place very frequently in the parliament
of England, where among the commons, the
whole houſe is formed on certain occaſions, into
a committee, for the better enquiry into, and
diſcuſſion of the matter in hand ; the members
become mere commiſſioners of the ſovereign
court they conſtituted but a moment before.
Agreeable to which, the enquiry being ended,
they make a report to themſelves, as the houſe
of Commons, of their proceedings as a grand
com-

committee, and deliberate anew under the former title on what they had already determined under the latter.

Such, indeed, is the peculiar advantage of a democratical government, that it is eftablifhed in fact by the fimple act of the general will. After which, this provifional government continues, if fuch be the intended form ; or eftablifhes, in the name of the fovercign, the form of government adopted by law ; and thus every thing proceeds according to order. It is impoffible to inftitute a government in any other legal manner, without renouncing the principles before eftablifhed.

CHAP. XVIII.

Of the means of preventing the ufurpations of government.

FROM the foregoing illuftrations refults the confirmation of what is afferted in the XVIth chapter, viz. that the act which infti-tutes government is not a contract but a law ; that the depofitories of the executive power are

not the mafters, but the fervants of the people ;
that the people may appoint or remove them
at pleafure ;. that they have no pretence to a contract with the people, but are bound to obey
them ; and that in accepting the offices the
ftate impofes on them, they only difcharge
their duty as citizens, without having any fort
of right to difpute the conditions.

When it fo happens, therefore, that the
people eftablifh an hereditary government,
whether monarchical, and confined to one
particular family, or ariftocratical, and divided
among a certain order of citizens, they do not
enter thereby into any formal engagement ; they
only give the adminiftration a provifional foim,
which remains legal till they think proper to
change it.

It is certain that fuch changes are always
dangerous, and that a government once eftablifhed fhould not be meddled with, unlefs it
be found incompatible with the public good ;
but this circumfpection is a maxim of policy,
and not a matter of right. The ftate, however, is no more bound to refign the civil authority

thority into the hands of its magiſtrates or
chiefs, than ·the military authority into thoſe
of its generals.

It is certain, alſo, that great care ſhould be
taken to obſerve all thoſe formalities, which, in
ſuch a caſe, are requiſite to diſtinguiſh a regular
and legal act from a ſeditious commotion ; to
diſtinguiſh between the general will of a whole
people and the clamours of a faction. In which
latter caſe, a people are particularly obliged to
give the beſt founded remonſtrances no farther
countenance, than in the utmoſt ſtrictneſs of
juſtice they may deſerve. Of this obligation,
however, the prince may take great advantages,
in order to preſerve his power in ſpite of the
people, without running the riſk of being
charged with uſurping it. For in appearing
only to make uſe of his prerogatives, he may
extend them, and under the pretence of maintaining the public peace, may prevent thoſe
aſſemblies which might otherwiſe be calculated
to re-eſtabliſh the good order of government :
ſo that he might profit by that ſilence which
he keeps from being broken, and by thoſe ir-

I 4 regu-

regularities which he himſelf might cauſe to
be committed ; pleading in his favour the tacit approbation of thoſe whoſe fears keep them
ſilent ; and puniſhing thoſe who are bold
enough to ſpeak. It was thus the *decemviri,*
at firſt elected for one year only, and afterwards continued for another, attempted to perpetuate the duration of their power, by preventing the *Comitia* from aſſembling as uſual ;
and it is by ſuch eaſy means that all the governments in the world, when once inveſted
with power, uſurp ſooner or later the ſovereign
authority.

Thoſe periodical aſſemblies, of which I
have ſpoken above, are very proper to prevent,
or protract, this misfortune, particularly when
they require no formal convocation ; for then
the prince cannot prevent them without de ·
claring himſelf openly a violator of the laws,
and an enemy to the ſtate.

The opening of theſe aſſemblies, which have
no other object than the preſervation of the
ſocial contract, ought always to be made by
two

two propositions, which can never be suppressed, and should pass separately by vote.

FIRST; Whether it be the determination of the sovereign to preserve the present form of government.

SECOND; Whether it be the determination of the people to continue the administration in the hands of those, who are at present charged with it.

It is to be observed, that I here take for granted, what I conceive has already been demonstrated, viz. that there is no fundamental law in any state, which such state cannot repeal, not excepting even the social compact: for, should all the citizens assemble with one accord to break this compact, it would undoubtedly be very legally dissolved. Grotius even thinks that an individual may renounce the state of which he is a member, and resume his natural independence and property by leaving the country *. Now it would be very

* With this exception, however, that he does not fly, to elude his duty, and avoid serving his coun-

I 5   try

very abfurd to fuppofe that the whole body
of citizens united. could not do that in concert, which any one of them might do feparately.

try on any emergency, when his fervice is required.
In this cafe his flight would be criminal and highly
deferving of punifhment. It would not be a retreat
but defertion.

The END of the THIRD BOOK.

BOOK

BOOK IV.

CHAP. I.

That the general will cannot be annihilated.

SO long as a number of individuals remain
perfectly united and confider themfelves as
one body, they can have but one will; which
relates to their common prefervation and wel-
fare. All the refources of the ftate, are then
fimple and vigorous, its political maxims clear
and obvious; it comprehends no intricate and
oppofite interefts; but that of the public is
demonftrably evident to all, and requires only
the gift of common fenfe to underftand it.
Peace, concord, and equality are enemies to political refinements. When men are honeft, and
fimple, their very fimplicity prevents their de-
ception; they are not to be impofed on by
fophiftry, but are too artlefs even to be duped.
When it is known, that, among the happieft
people in the world, a number of peafants meet
together under the fhade of an oak, and regulate the affairs of ftate, with the moft pru-
dential œconomy, is it poffible to forbear de-

I 6   *fpifing*

fpifing the refinements of other nations, who
employ fo much artifice and myftery to render
themfelves fplendidly miferable ?

A ftate thus fimply governed hath need of
but few laws, while in proportion as it becomes
neceffary to promulgate new ones, that neceffity
is univerfally apparent. The firft perfon who
propofes them, takes on himfelf to fpeak only
what every one hath already thought; and neither eloquence nor intrigue is requifite to make
that pafs into a law, which every one had already refolved to do, as foon as he fhould be
affured others would do the fame.

That which deceives our reafoners on this
fubject, is, that, feeing none but fuch ftates as
were badly conftituted at their beginning, they
are ftruck with the impoffibility of maintaining
fuch a police in them. They fmile to think of
the abfurdities, into which a defigning knave
or infinuating orator might lead the people of
Paris and London. They are not apprized that
a Cromwell, and a Beaufort, would have been
treated as incendiaries at Berne and Geneva,
and have underwent the difcipline due to their
demerit.

But

But when the bonds of fociety begin to relax, and the ftate to grow weak ; when the private interefts of individuals begin to appear, and that of parties to influence the ftate, the objects of public good meet with oppofition ; unanimity no longer prefides in the affemblies of the people ; the general will is no longer the will of all ; contradictions and debates arife, and the moft falutary counfel is not adopted without difpute.

Again, when the ftate is bordering on ruin, and exifts only in empty form, when the focial tie no longer connects the hearts of the people, when the bafeft motives of intereft impudently affume the facred name of the public good ; then is the general will altogether filent ; individuals, actuated by private motives, cherifh no more the fentiments of citizens, than if the ftate had never exifted, while the mock legiflature pafs, under the name of laws, thofe iniquitous decrees which have no other end than private intereft.

Doth it follow from hence, however, that the general will is annihilated or corrupted ? No. This remains ever conftant, invariable, and

and pure ; though it is fubjected to that of party.
There is not an individual who doth not fee,
while he detaches his own intereft from that
of the public, that he cannot feparate himfelf
from it entirely : but his fhare in the common
evil feems nothing in comparifon to the good
which he propofes to fecure exclufively to himfelf. Setting this motive afide he is as ready
to concur in meafures for the good of the public, and that even for his own fake as any one.
Nay. even in felling his vote, he doth not lofe
all fenfe of the general will, he only eludes it.
The fault he is guilty of, lies in changing the
ftate of the queftion, and making an anfwer to
what is not afked him ; fo that, inftead of ad-
mitting by his vote, *that it is to the intereft of
the ftate*. he fays, *it is to the intereft of fuch an
individual or fuch a party, that this or that law
fhould pafs* Thus the order which fhould prevail in the public affemblies of the ftate, fhould
not be calculated fo much to preferve the general will inviolate, as to caufe it to be always
interrogated, and to make it anfwer.

I might here make a variety of reflections
on the fimple right of voting in every act of
the fovereignty ; a right which the citizens
cannot be deprived of : as alfo on the rights of
think-

thinking, propofing and debating on public matters; privileges which government is ever folicitous enough to confine to its own members. This fubject, however, is of importance enough to deferve a whole treatife of itfelf; and it is impoffible for me to fay every thing in the prefent.

CHAP. II.

On Votes.

IT is evident, from what hath been faid in the preceding chapter, that the manner in which public affairs are carried on, may afford a fure indication of the actual ftate of manners, and the health of the body politic. The more concord there is in public affemblies, that is to fay, the nearer the members approach to unanimity in giving their votes, the more prevalent is the general will among them: but long debates, diffentions and commotions, evince the afcendency of particular interefts and the decline of the ftate.

This appears lefs evident, indeed, when two or more orders of men, enter into the conftitution; as at Rome, where the quarrels of the
Pa-

Patricians and Plebeians occafioned frequent di-
fturbances in the *Comitia*, even in the moft flourifhing times of the republic.   This exception
however, is more apparent than real : as in that
cafe there exifts, by a defect inherent in the
body politic, two ftates in one ; and that which
is not true of both together, may neverthelefs
be true of each apart.   It is alfo true in fact
that, even during the moft turbulent times of
the republic, the decrees of the Plebeians, when
he Senate did not intermeddle, were paffed
with great tranquillity agreeable to the plurality of voices.   The citizens having but one
common intereft, the people could have but one
will.

Unanimity returns again at the oppofite ex-
tremity of the circle ; and this is where the citizens, reduced to flavery, have neither liberty
nor will.   In fuch a fituation, fear and flattery
pervert their votes into acclamations ; they no
longer deliberate among themfelves ; but either
adore or curfe their tyrants.   Such were the
debafed principles of the Senate under the Roman emperors.   Under thefe circumftances alfo,
the fentiments of the public were frequently
expreffed, with the moft ridiculous precau-
tion ; Tacitus obferving that, under Otho, the
Se-

Senators, while they loaded Vitellius with exe-
crations, they affected at the same time to
make a confused and clamorous noise, in order
to prevent his knowing, should he become
their master, what any individual had said.

From these considerations may be deduced
the maxims, on which the manner of counting
votes, and comparing different suffrages, should
be regulated, according as the general will is more
or less easy to be discovered, and the state more
or less advanced towards its decline. There is
but one law, which in its own nature, requires
unanimous consent: and this is the social compact. For civil association is the most voluntary act in the world : every man being born
free, and master of himself, no one can lay him
under restraint, on any pretence whatever,
without his own consent. To affirm that the
son of a slave is born a slave, is to affirm he is
not born a man.

If there be any persons, however, who oppose this contract itself, their opposition does
not invalidate that contract; it only hinders
their being comprehended therein ; and they remain aliens in the midst of citizens. When
a state

a ſtate is formed, a conſent to its inſtitution is inferred by the reſidence of the party : to ſub-- mit to reſidence in any country is to ſubmit to its ſovereignty *.

If we except this primitive contract, the determination of the majority is always obligatory on the reſt : this is a neceſſary conſequence of the contract itſelf. But it may be aſked, how can a man be free, and yet be obliged to conform to the will of others. How can the members of an oppoſition be called free-men, who are compelled to ſubmit to laws which they have not conſented to ? I anſwer that this queſtion is not properly ſtated. The citizen conſents to all laws paſſed by a majority, though ſome of them in particular may have paſſed contrary to his inclination ; nay he conſents to thoſe by which he is puniſhable for the breach of

* This muſt always be underſtood, however, of a free ſtate, from which people have the liberty to depart with their effects at pleaſure. For in others the conſideration of their family, their property, the want of an aſylum, neceſſity or violence, may detain an inhabitant in a country contrary to his will; in which caſe, his ſimple reſidence neither implies his conſent to the contract, nor his violation of it.

any

any one. The conftant will of all the members of a ftate, is the general will ; and it is
this alone that makes them either citizens or
freemen *. When a law is propofed in the
affembly of the people, they are not precifely
demanded, whether they feverally approve or
reject the propofition ; but whether it be conformable or not to the general will, which is
theirs as a collective body ; each perfon, therefore, in giving his vote declares his opinion on
this head, and on counting the votes, the declaration of the general will, is inferred from
the majority. When a law thus paffes contrary
to my opinion, it proves nothing more than
that I was miftaken, and that I concluded the
general will to be what it really was not. So
that, if my particular advice had been followed, it would have been contrary to my will,

* At Genoa we fee the word *Libertas* infcribed
on the chains of the galley flaves, and on the doors
of the prifoners : the application of which device is
beautiful and juft ; as it is in fact only the criminals
of all ftates that infringe the liberty of the citizen.
A country, whofe malefactors fhould be all actually
chained to the oar, would be a country of the moft
perfect liberty.

which

which as a citizen is the fame as the general, and in that cafe I fhould not have been free.

This argument fuppofes, indeed, that all the characteriftics of the general will, are contained in the plurality of votes: and when this ceafes to be the cafe, take what courfe you will, there is an end of liberty.

In having fhewn how the will of particulars and parties is fubftituted for the general, in public deliberations, I have already fufficiently pointed out the practicable means of preventing fuch abufes; of this, however, I fhall fpeak further hereafter. With regard to the proportional number of votes that indicate this general will, I have alfo laid down the principles on which it may be determined. The difference of a fingle voice is enough to break the unanimity; but between unanimity and an equality there is a variety of proportions; to each of which the number in queftion may be applied, according to the circumftances of the body politic.

There are two general maxims, which may ferve to regulate thefe proportions: the one is, that the more grave and important the deliberations, the

the nearer ought the determination to approach to unanimity : .the other is, that the more expedition the affair requires, the lefs fhould unanimity be infifted on. In deliberations where the matter fhould be immediately determined, the majority of a fingle vote fhould be fufficient. The firft of thefe maxims feems moft applicable to permanent laws, and the fecond to matters of bufinefs. But be this as it may, it is from their judicious combination, that the beft proportions muft be deduced, concerning that plurality in whofe votes fhould be fuppofed to confift the general will.

C H A P. III.

Of Elections.

WITH regard to the election of a prince or of magiftrates, which, as I before obferved is a complicated act; there are two methods of proceeding ; viz. by choice and by lot. They have each been made ufe of in different republics; and we fee in our own times, a very intricate mixture of both in the election of the doge of Venice.

The

The preference by lot, fays Montefquieu, *is of the nature of a democracy.* This I admit, but not for the reafons given. *The choice by lot*, fays he, *is a method which offends no-body ; by permitting each citizen to entertain the reafonable hope of being preferred to the fervice of his country.*

This, however, is not the true reafon. If we reflect that the election of chiefs is a function of government and not of the fovereignty, we fhall fee the reafon why this method is of the nature of a democracy, in which the adminiftration is fo much the better, as its acts are fewer.

In every real democracy the office of magiftrate is not advantageous but expenfive and burthenfome, fo that it were unjuft to impofe it on one perfon rather than another. The law, therefore, impofes that charge on him, to whofe lot it falls. For in this cafe, all ftanding an equal chance, the choice doth not depend on human will, nor can any particular application change the univerfality of the law.

In an ariftocracy the prince makes choice of the prince ; and, the government providing for
it-

itſelf, here it is that votes are properly applicable. The apparent exception, in the election of the doge of Venice, confirms this diſtinction, inſtead of deſtroying it : ſuch a mixt form as is uſed by the Venetians is adapted to a mixt government. For it is a miſtake to ſuppoſe the government of Venice a true ariſtocracy. If the lower order of people, indeed, have no ſhare in the government, the nobility ſtand in their place, and become the people in reſpect to the adminiſtration. What a number is there of the inferior order of nobles, who ſtand no chance of ever getting into the magiſtracy,, and reap no other advantage from their rank than the empty title of Excellency, and the privilege of ſitting in the great Council. - This great council being as numerous as our general council at Geneva, its illuſtrious members have no greater privileges therefore than our ordinary citizens. It is certain, that ſetting aſide the extreme diſparity of the two republics, the burghers of Geneva repreſent exactly the Patricians of Venice ; our natives and ſojourners repreſent the citizens and people, and our peaſants the inhabitants of the *terra firma* belonging to that ſtate. In a word, conſider their Venetian republic in what light you will,

will, abftracted from its grandeur, its go·
vernment, is no more ariftocratical than that of
Geneva. All the difference is that we have no
occafion for this kind of election.

The choice by lot, is attended with very little
inconvenience in a real democracy, when all men
being nearly on an equality, as well with regard
to manners and abilities, as to fentiments
and fortune, the matter of choice is indifferent.
But I have already obferved a true democracy is
only imaginary.

When the election is of a mixt form, viz.
by vote and by lot, the firft ought to provide
for thofe officers which require proper talents,
as in military affairs; the other being beft adapted to thofe which require only common fenfe,
honefty and integrity; fuch as the offices of
judicature; becaufe in a well-formed ftate, thofe
qualities are poffeffed by all the citizens in
common.

No election either by vote or lot, hath place
under a monarchical government; the monarch
himfelf being the only rightful prince and legal
magiftrate, the choice of his fubftitute is vefted
in

in him alone. When the Abbé de St. Pierre, therefore, propofed to increafe the number of the king's councils in France, and to elect their members by ballot, he was not aware that he propofed to change the form of the French go- vernment.

It remains to fpeak of the manner of giving and collecting votes in popular affemblies; but, perhaps, an hiftorical fketch of the Roman po- lice relating to this point, will explain it better than all the maxims I fhould endeavour to efta- blifh. It is worth the pains of a judicious rea- der, to attend a little particularly to the man- ner, in which they treated affairs, both general and particular, in a council of two hundred thoufand perfons.

K   C H A P.

CHAP. IV.

Of the Roman Comitia.

WE have no authentic monuments of the earliest ages of Rome; there is even great reason to believe that most of the stories told us of them are fabulous*; and indeed, the most interesting and instructive part of the annals of nations in general, which is that of their establishment, is the most imperfect. Experience daily teaches us to what causes are owing the revolutions of kingdoms and empires; but as we see no instances of the original formation of states, we can only proceed on conjectures in treating this subject.

The customs we find actually established, however, sufficiently attest, there must have been an origin of those customs. Those traditions,

---

* The name of *Rome*, which it is pretended was taken from *Romulus*, is Greek, and signifies *force*; the name of Numa is Greek also, and signifies *law*. What probability is there that the two first kings of this city should have been called by names so expressive of their future actions?

alſo,

alfo, relating to fuch origin, which appear the moſt rational, and of the beſt authority ought to paſs for the moſt certain. Theſe are the maxims I have adopted in tracing the manner in which the moſt powerful and free people in the univerſe, exerciſed the fovereign authority.

After the foundation of Rome, the riſing republic, that is to fay, the army of the founder, compoſed of Albans, Sabines and foreigners, was divided into three claſſes; which, from that diviſion, took the name of tribes. Each of theſe tribes was fubdivided into ten *Curiæ*, and each *Curia* into *decuriæ*, at the head of which were placed chiefs reſpectively denominated *curiones* and *decuriones*.

Befide this, there were felected from each tribe a body of an hundred cavaliers or knights, called *centurions*; by which it is evident that theſe diviſions, not being eſſential to the good order of a city, were at firſt only military. But it feems as if the prefaging inſtinct of future greatneſs, induced the little town of Rome to adopt at firſt a ſyſtem of police proper for the metropolis of the world.

From

From this primitive divifion, however, there fpeedily refulted an inconvenience. This was that the tribe of Albans, and that of the Sabines always remaining the fame, while that of the ftrangers was perpetually encreafing by the concourfe of foreigners, the latter foon furpaffed the number of the two former. The remedy which Servius applied to correct this dangerous abufe was to change the divifion; and to fub-ftitute, in the room of diftinction of race, which he abolifhed, another taken from the parts of the town occupied by each tribe. Inftead of three tribes, he conftituted four; each of which occupied one of the hills of Rome, and bore its name. Thus by removing this inequality for the prefent, he prevented it alfo for the future; and in order that fuch divifion fhould not only be local but perfonal, he prohibited the inhabitants of one quarter of the city, from removing to the other, and thereby prevented the mixture of families.

He doubled alfo the three ancient centuries of cavalry, and made an addition of twelve others, but always under their old denomination; a fimple and judicious method, by which he compleatly diftinguifhed the body of knights from

from that of the people, without exciting the murmurs of the latter.

Again, to thefe four city tribes, Servius added fifteen others, called ruftic tribes, becaufe they were formed of the inhabitants of the country, divided into as many cantons. In the fequel were made an equal number of new divifions, and the Roman people found themfelves divided into thirty-five tribes; the number at which their divifions remained fixed, till the final diffolution of the republic.

From the diftinction between the tribes of city and country, refulted an effect worthy of obfervation; becaufe we have no other example of it, and becaufe Rome was at once indebted to it for the prefervation of its manners and the increafe of its empire. It might be conceived the city tribes would foon arrogate to themfelves, the power and honours of the ftate, and treat the ruftics with contempt. The effect, nevertheless, was directly contrary. The tafte of the ancient Romans for a country life is well known. They derived this tafte from the wife inftitutor, who joined to liberty the labours of the peafant and the foldier, and configned, as

K 3   it

it were, to the city, the cultivation of the arts, trade, intrigue, fortune and flavery.

Thus the moft illuftrious perfonages of Rome, living in the country, and employing themfelves in the bufinefs of agriculture, it was among thefe only the Romans looked for the defenders of their republic. This ftation, being that of the moft worthy patricians, was held in univerfal efteem : the fimple and laborious life of the villager was preferred to the mean and lazy life of the citizen; and a perfon who, having been a labourer in the country, became a refpectable houfe-keeper in town, was yet held in contempt.   It is with reafon, fays Varro, that our magnanimous anceftors eftablifhed in the country the nurfery for thofe robuft and brave men, who defended them in time of war and cherifhed them in peace.   Again, Pliny fays in exprefs terms, the country tribes were honoured becaufe of the perfons of which they were compofed ; whereas fuch of their individuals as were to be treated with ignominy, were removed into the tribes of the city.   When the Sabine, Appius Claudius, came to fettle in Rome, he was loaded with honours, and regiftered in one of the ruftic tribes, which afterwards took

the

the name of his family. Laftly, the freed-men
were all entered in the city tribes, never in the
rural ; nor is there one fingle inftance, during
the exiftence of the republic, of any one of
thefe freedmen being preferred to the magiftracy, although become a citizen.

This was an excellent maxim, but was carried fo far, that it effected an alteration, and undoubtedly an abufe in the police of the ftate.

In the firft place, the Cenfors, after having
long arrogated the right of arbitrarily removing
the citizens from one tribe to another, permitted the greater part to regifter themfelves
in whatever tribe they pleafed ; a permiffion
that could furely anfwer no good end, and yet
it deprived thefe officers of one of their fevereft
methods of cenfure. Befides, as the great and
powerful thus got themfelves regiftered in the
rural tribes ; and the freedmen, with the populace, only filled up thofe of the city ; the
tribes in general had no longer a local diftinction : but were fo ftrangely mixed and jumbled
together, that their refpective members could
be known only by appealing to the regifters ;
fo that the idea attached to the word tribe,

was

was changed from real to perfonal, or rather became altogether chimerical.

It happened alfo that the tribes of the city, being nearer at hand, had generally the greateft influence in the *Comitia*, and made a property of the ftate, by felling their votes to thofe who were bafe enough to purchafe them.

With regard to the *Curiæ*, ten having been inftituted in each tribe, the whole Roman people, included within the walls, made up thirty *Curiæ*, each of which had their peculiar temples, their gods, officers and feafts called *Compitalia*, refembling the *paganalia*, afterwards inftituted among the ruftic tribes.

At the new divifion made by Servius, the number thirty not being equally divifible among the four tribes, he forbore to meddle with this mode of diftribution ; and the Curiæ, thus independent of the tribes, formed another divifion of the inhabitants. No notice, however, was taken of the Curiæ, either among the ruftic tribes, or the people compofing them ; becaufe the tribes becoming a mere civil eftablifhment, and another method having been introduced for
raifing

raifing the troops, the military diftinctions of Romulus were dropt as fuperfluous. Thus, though every citizen was regiftered in fome tribe, yet many of them were not included in any *curia*. Servius made ftill a third divifion, which had no relation to the two former, and became in its confequences the moft important of all. He divided the whole Roman people into fix claffes, which he diftinguifhed, neither by perfons nor place, but by property. Of thefe the higher claffes were filled by the rich, the lower by the poor, and the middle claffes by thofe of middling fortunes. Thefe fix claffes were fubdivided into one hundred ninety-three other bodies called centuries; and thefe were again fo diftributed that the firft clafs alone comprehended more than half the number of centuries, and the laft clafs only one fingle century. In this method the clafs that contained the feweft perfons, had the greater number of centuries; and the laft clafs was in number only a fubdivifion, although it contained more than half the inhabitants of Rome.

In order that the people fhould penetrate lefs into the defign of this latter form of diftribution, Servius affected to give it the air of a mi-

litary

litary one. In the fecond clafs he incorporated
two centuries of armourers, and annexed two
inftruments of war to the fourth.   In each
clafs, except the laft, he diftinguifhed alfo between the young and the old, that is to fay,
thofe who were obliged to bear arms, from thofe
who were exempted from it on account of their
age ; a diftinction which gave more frequent
rife to the repetition of the *cenfus* or enumera-
tion of them, than even the fhifting of property : laftly, he required their affembly to be made
on the *Campus Martius*, where all thofe who
were of age for the fervice were to appear under
arms.

The reafon, why he did not purfue the fame
diftinction of age in the laft clafs, was, that the
populace, of which it was compofed, were not
permitted to have the honour of bearing arms
in the fervice of their country.   It was neceffary
to be houfe-keepers, in order to attain the privilege of defending themfelves. There is not one
private centinel perhaps, of all thofe innumer-
able troops, that make fo brilliant a figure in
the armies of modern princes, who would not,
for want of property, have been driven out
with difdain from a Roman Cohort, when foldiers were the defenders of liberty.

In

In the laft clafs, however, there was a diftinction made between what they called *proletarii* and
thofe denominated *capite cenfi*. The former,
not quite reduced to nothing, fupplied the ftate
at leaft with citizens, and fometimes on prefling
occafions with foldiers. As to thofe, who were
totally deftitute of fubftance, and could be
numbered only by capitation, they were difregarded as nothing ; Marius being the firft who
deigned to enroll them.

Without taking upon me here to decide, whether this third fpecies of divifion be in itfelf
good or ill ; I may venture fafely to affirm, that
nothing lefs than that fimplicity of manners,
which prevailed among the ancient Romans,
their difinereftednefs, their tafte for agriculture, their contempt for trade and the thirft of
gain, could have rendered it practicable. Where
is the nation among the moderns, in which voracious avarice, a turbulence of difpofition, a
fpirit of artifice, and the continual fluctuation
of property, would permit fuch an eftablifhment to continue for twenty years without over-
turning the ftate ? Nay it muft be well obferved
that the purity of the Roman manners, and the
force of a cenfure more efficacious than the in-

ftitution

ftitution itfelf, ferved to correct the defects of
it at Rome, where a rich man was often removed from his own clafs and ranked among the
poor, for making an improper parade of his
wealth.

It is eafy to comprehend from this, why mention is hardly ever made of more than five claffes,
though there were in reality fix. The fixth,
furnifhing neither the army with foldiers, nor
the *Campus Martius* * with voters, and being
of hardly any ufe in the republic, was hardly
ever accounted any thing.

Such were the different divifions of the Roman people. We will now examine into the defects, of which they were productive, in their
affemblies. Thefe affemblies, when legally con-
voked, were denominated *Comitia*, and were held
in the *Campus Martius* and other parts of Rome ;
being diftinguifhed into *curiata*, *centuriata*, and
tributa, according to the three grand divifions

* I fay the *Campus Martius*, becaufe it was there
the *Comitia* affembled by centuries ; in the two other
forms, they affembled in the *forum* and other places,
where the *capite cenfi* had as much influence and importance as the principal citizens.

of

of the people into *Curiæ*, *Centuries*, and *Tribes*. The *Comitia curiata* were inflituted by Romulus, the *Centuriata* by Servius, and the *Tributa* by the tribunes of the people. Nothing could pafs into a law, nor could any magiftrate be chofen but in the *Comitia*, and as there was no citizen who was not enrolled in a *Curia*, *Century* or *Tribe*, it follows that no citizen was excluded from giving his vote; fo that the Roman people were truly fovereign both in right and fact.

To make the affembly of the *Comitia* legal, and give their determinations the force of laws, three conditions were requifite. In the firft place it was neceffary that the magiftrate or body convoking them, fhould be invefted with proper authority for fo doing: Secondly, that the affembly fhould occur on the days permitted by law; and thirdly, that the augurs fhould be favourable to their meeting.

The reafon of the firft condition needs no explanation: The fecond is an affair of police; thus it was not permitted the *Comitia* to affemble on market days, when the country people, coming to Rome on bufinefs, would be pre-, vented from tranfacting it. By the third, the Senate kept a fierce and turbulent multitude

6   under

under fome reftraint, and opportunely checked
the ardour of the feditious tribunes; the latter,
however, found more ways than one to elude
the force of this expedient.

But the laws and the election of the chiefs
were not the only matters fubmitted to the determination of the *Comitia:* the Roman people
having ufurped the moft important functions of
government, the fate of Europe might be faid
to depend on their affemblies. Hence the variety of objects that came before them, gave
occafion for divers alterations in the form of
thefe affemblies, according to the nature of thofe
objects.

To judge of thefe diverfities, it is fufficient
to compare them together. The defign of Romulus in inftituting the *Curiæ*, was to reftrain
the Senate by means of the people, and the
people by the Senate, while he himfelf maintained his influence equally over both. By this
form, therefore, he gave to the people all the
authority of number to counterballance that of
power and riches, which he left in the hands
of the Patricians. But, agreeable to the fpirit
of monarchy, he gave more advantage to the
Patricians, by the influence of their clients to obtain

tain the majority of votes. This admirable institution of patrons and clients, was a master-
piece of politics and humanity, without which
the order of Patricians, so contrary to the spirit
of the republic, could not have subsisted. Rome
alone hath the honour of giving to the world
this fine example, of which no abuse is known
to have been made, and which nevertheless hath
never been adopted by other nations.

This division by *Curiæ* having subsisted under
the kings till the time of Servius, and the reign
of the last *Tarquin* being accounted illegal, the
regal laws came hence to be generally distinguished by the name of *leges curiatæ*.

Under the republic, the *Curiæ*, always confined to the four city tribes, and comprehending only the populace of Rome, could not arrive either at the honour of sitting in the Senate, which was at the head of the Patricians,
or at that of being Tribunes, which, notwith-
standing they were Plebeians, were yet at the
head of the citizens in easy circumstances. They
fell, therefore, into discredit, and were reduced to so contemptible a state that their thirty
Lictors assembled to do the whole business of
the *Comitia curiata*.

The

The divifion by *centuries*, was fo favourable to ariftocracy, that it is not at firft eafy to comprehend why the Senate did not always carry their point in the *Comitia centuriata*, by which the Confuls, Cenfors, and Prætors were chofen. It is in fact certain that out of the hundred and ninety three centuries, forming the fix claffes of the whole Roman people, the firft clafs containing ninety eight of them, and the votes being reckoned only centuries, this firft clafs alone had more votes than all the others. When the centuries of this clafs, therefore, were found to be unanimous, they proceeded no farther in counting votes; whatever might be determined by the minority being confidered as the opinion of the mob. So that it might be juftly faid, that in the *Comitia centuriata* matters were carried rather by the greater quantity of money, than the majority of votes.

But this extreme authority was moderated by two caufes. In the firft place, the Tribunes, generally fpeaking, and always a confiderable number of wealthy citizens, being in this clafs of the rich, they counterpoized the credit of the Patricians in the fame clafs. The fecond caufe lay in the manner of voting, which was this; the centuries, inftead of voting according

to

to order, beginning with the firſt in rank, caſt lots which ſhould proceed firſt to the election. And to this the century whoſe lot it was, proceeded * alone; the other centuries being called upon another day to give their votes according to their rank, when they repeated the ſame election, and uſually confirmed the choice of the former. By this method the preference of rank was ſet aſide, in order to give it according to lot, agreeable to the principles of democracy.

There is another advantage reſulting from this cuſtom; which is that the citizens reſiding in the country had time between the two elections to inform themſelves of the merit of the candidates thus proviſionally nominated; by which means they might be better enabled to give their vote. But under the pretence of expediting affairs, this cuſtom was in time aboliſhed, and the two elections were made the ſame day.

* The century thus preferred by lot was called *præ rogativa*; becauſe it was the firſt whoſe ſuffrage was demanded; and hence is derived the word *prerogative*.

The

The *Comitia by Tribes*, were properly speaking the great council of the Roman people. These were convoked only by the Tribunes; by these also the Tribunes were chosen, and by these the *plebiscita* or laws of the people were passed. The Senators were not only destitute of rank in these assemblies; they had not even the right to be present at them; but, obliged to pay obedience to laws in the enacting of which they had no vote, they were in that respect less free than the lowest citizens. This injustice, however, was very ill understood, and was in itself alone sufficient to invalidate the decrees of a body, whose members were not all admitted to vote. Had all the Patricians assisted at these *Comitia*, as they had a right, in quality of citizens, they could have had no undue influence where every man's vote was equal, even from the lowest of the people to the highest personage of the state.

It is evident, therefore, that, exclusive of the good order that resulted from these several divisions, in collecting the votes of so numerous a people, the form and method of these divisions were not indifferent in themselves; each being productive of effects, adapted to
certain

certain views in regard to which it was preferable to any other.

But without entering into a more circumstantial account of these matters, it is plain from what hath been advanced, that the *Comitia tribunata* were the most favourable to a popular government, and the *Comitia centuriata* to an aristocracy. With respect to the *Comitia curiata* of which the populace formed the majority, as they were good for nothing but to favour tyrannical designs, they remained in this contemptible state, into which they were fallen; even the contrivers of sedition themselves not chusing to employ means, which must have exposed too openly their designs. It is very certain that all the majesty of the Roman people was displayed only in the *Comitia centuriata*, which only were compleat; the *curiata* wanting the rustic Tribes, and the *tribunata* the Senate and Patricians.

With regard to the method of collecting the votes, it was, among the primitive Romans, simple as their manners, though still less simple than that of Sparta. Every one gave his vote aloud, which the register took down in writing; the plurality of votes in each tribe, determined the vote of that tribe, and the plurality of votes in the tribes

tribes determined the suffrage of the people. In the same manner also they proceeded with regard to the *Curiæ* and the centuries. This custom was a very good one, so long as integrity prevailed among the citizens, and every one was ashamed to give his public sanction to an unworthy person or cause. But when the people grew corrupt and sold their votes, it became necessary to make them give their votes more privately, in order to restrain the purchasers by distrust, and afford knaves an expedient to avoid being traitors.

I know that Cicero censures this alteration, and attributes to it in a great degree the ruin of the republic. But, though I am sensible of all the weight of Cicero's authority in this case, I cannot be of his opinion. I conceive, on the contrary, that the ruin of the state would have been accelerated, had the Romans neglected making this alteration. As the regimen of people in health, is not proper for the sick, so it is absurd to think of governing a corrupt people by the same laws as were expedient for them before they were corrupted. There cannot be a stronger proof of this maxim, than the duration of the republic of Venice, the shadow of which still exists, solely because its laws are adapted only to bad men.

On

On this change in the manner of voting, ta-
blets were diftributed among the citizens, by
means of which they could give their fuffrage
without its being known   On this occafion
other methods were of courfe made ufe of in
collecting votes, fuch as counting the number
of voices, comparing it with that of the ta-
blets, &c. Not that thefe methods were fo
effectual as - to prevent the returning officers *
from being often fufpected of partiality : and it
is plain in the fequel, by the multiplicity of
laws made to prevent bribery and corruption
in elections, that they could not effect this
point.

Toward the decline of the republic, recourfe
was had to very extraordinary expedients, to
make up for the infufficiency of the laws.   Pro-
digies were fometimes played off with fuccefs ;
but this fcheme, though it impofed on the multitude, did not impofe on thofe who influenced
them.   Sometimes affemblies were called fud-
denly, and in great hafte, that the candidates
might not have time to create an undue intereft :
at others again the whole feffions was fpent in
declamation, when it was feen that the people

* Cuftodes, ditibitores, rogatores, fuffragiorum.

were

were biaffed to take a wrong fide. At length, however, ambition eluded all thefe precautions, and it is almoft incredible that, in the midft of fo many abufes, this immenfe people ftill continued, by virtue of their ancient laws, to elect their magiftrates, to pafs laws, to judge caufes, and to expedite both public and private affairs, with as much facility as could have been done in the Senate itfelf.

C H A P. V.

On a Tribunate.

WHEN it is impracticable to eftablifh an exact proportion between the component parts of a ftate, or that inevitable caufes perpetually operate to change their relations, a particular magiftracy is inftituted which, not incorporating with the reft, replaces every term in its true relation, and conftitutes in itfelf a due medium either between the prince and the people, between the prince and the fovereign, or, in cafes of neceffity, at once between both.

This body, which I fhall call a *Tribunate*, is the preferver of the laws and of the legiflative power.

power. It serves sometimes to protect the sovereign against the government, as the tribunes of the people did at Rome; sometimes to protect the government against the people, as at present the council of the *ten* do at Venice; and again at others to maintain an equilibrium both on the one part and the other, as did the Ephori at Sparta.

The Tribunate is not a constitutional part of the city, and ought not, therefore, to have any share in the legislative or executive power: even in this however, its own is much greater: for being able to do nothing itself, it may prevent any thing from being done by others. It is more sacred and revered, as defender of the laws, than the prince who executes them, or the sovereign who enacts them. This was very evident at Rome, when the haughty Patricians, who always despised the people collectively, were nevertheless obliged to give place to their common officers, without command or jurisdiction.

The Tribunate when judiciously moderated is the firmest support of a good constitution; but if it have ever so little ascendency of power,

it

it fubverts every thing. With regard to its weaknefs it is not natural to it ; for, provided it have any exiftence at all, it can never have too little power.

It degenerates into tyranny when it ufurps the executive power, of which it is only the moderator, and when it would interpret the laws which it fhould only protect. The enormous power of the Ephori, which was exercifed without danger, while Sparta retained its purity of manners, ferved only to increafe the corruption of them when once begun. The blood of Agis fpilt by thofe tyrants was revenged by his fucceffor : the crime and the punifhment of the Ephori accelerated equally the ruin of that republic; for after the time of Cleomenes Sparta was nothing. The deftruction of the Roman republic was effected in the fame manner : the exceffive power which the Tribunes by degrees ufurped, ferved at length, with the help of the laws made in defence of liberty, as a fecurity to the Emperors who deftroyed it. As for the council of *ten* at Venice ; it is a moft fanguinary tribunal, equally horrible to the Patricians and the people, and which is fo far from openly protecting the laws, that it now ferves but fecretly to effect the breach of them.

The

The Tribunate is enfeebled, as well as the government, by increasing the number of its members. When the Roman Tribunes, at firſt two, and afterwards five, had a mind to double their number, the Senate did not oppoſe it; being well aſſured they ſhould be able to make one a curb to another; which was actually the caſe.

The beſt way to prevent the uſurpations of ſo formidable a body, a way that no government hath hitherto adopted, would be to render ſuch a body not permanent, but to regulate the intervals during which it ſhould remain diſſolved. Theſe intervals which ſhould not be ſo great as to give abuſes time to ſtrengthen into cuſtoms, might be fixed by law, in ſuch a manner that it would be eaſy to abridge them, in caſe of neceſſity by extraordinary commiſſion.

This method appears to me, to be attended with no inconvenience; becauſe, as I have already obſerved, the Tribunate making no eſſential part of the conſtitution, may be ſuppreſſed without injury: and it appears to me effectual, becauſe a magiſtrate newly re-eſtabliſhed doth not ſucceed to the power of his predeceſſor, but to that which the law confers on him.

L   C H A P.

CHAP. VI.

Of the Dictature.

THAT inflexibility of the laws, which prevents their yielding to circumstances, may
in some cases render them hurtful, and in some
critical juncture bring on the ruin of the state.
The order and prolixity of forms, take up a
length of time, of which the occasion will not always admit. A thousand accidents may happen for which the legislature hath not provided ; and it is a very necessary foresight to see
that it is impossible to provide for every thing.

We should not be desirous, therefore, of
establishing the laws so firmly as to suspend their
effects. Even Sparta itself sometimes permitted
the laws to lie dormant.

Nothing, however, but the certainty of greater
danger should induce a people to make any alteration in government ; nor should the sacred
power of the laws be ever restrained unless the
public safety is concerned. In such uncommon
cases, when the danger is manifest, the public safety may be provided for by a particular act,
which commits the charge of it to those who
are

are moſt worthy. Such a commiſſion may paſs, in two different ways, according to the nature of the danger.

If the caſe require only a greater activity in the government, it ſhould be confined to one or two members; in which caſe it would not be the authority of the laws, but the form of the adminiſtration only that would be changed. But if the danger be of ſuch a nature, that the formality of the laws would prevent a remedy, then a ſupreme chief might be nominated who ſhould ſilence the laws, and ſuſpend for a moment the ſovereign authority. In ſuch a caſe, the general Will cannot be doubted, it being evident that the principal intention of the people muſt be to ſave the ſtate from perdition, By this mode of temporary ſuſpenſion the legiſlative authority is not aboliſhed; the magiſtrate who ſilences it, cannot make it ſpeak, and though he over-rules cannot repreſent it ; he may do every thing indeed but make laws.

The firſt method was taken by the Roman Senate, when it charged the conſuls, in a ſacred manner, to provide for the ſafety of the

com-

common-wealth. The second took place when one of the confuls nominated a dictator *; a cuftom which Rome adopted from the example of Alba.

In the early times of the republic, the Romans had frequent recourfe to the dictatorfhip, becaufe the ftate had not then fufficient ftability to fupport itfelf by the force of its conftitution. The manners of the people, alfo, rendering thofe precautions unneceffary, which were taken in after-times, there was no fear that a dictator would abufe his authority, or that he would be tempted to keep it in his hands, beyond the term. On the contrary, it appeared that fo great a power was burthenfome to the perfon invefted with it, fo eager were they to refign it; as if it were a difficult and dangerous poft, to be fuperior to the laws.

Thus it was not the danger of the abufe, but of the debafement of this fupreme magiftracy,

* This nomination was fecretly made in the night, as if they were afhamed of the action of placing any man fo much above the laws.

that

that gave occasion to censure the indiscreet use of it, in ancient times. For when they came to prostitute it in the affair of elections and other matters of mere formality, it was very justly to be apprehended that it would become less respectable on pressing occasions; and that the people would be apt to look upon an office as merely titular, which was instituted to assist at empty ceremonies.

Toward the end of the republic, the Romans, becoming more circumspect, were as sparing of the dictature, as they had before been prodigal of it. It was easy to see, however, that their fears were groundless, that the weakness of the capital was their security against the internal magistrates; that a dictator might in some cases have acted in defence of public liberty, without ever making encroachments on it; and that the Roman chains were not forged in Rome itself, but in its armies abroad. The weak resistance which Marius made to Sylla and Pompey to Cæsar, shewed plainly how little the authority from within the city could do against the power from without.

This error led them to commit great blun-
ders. Such for inftance, was their neglecting
to appoint a dictator in the affair of Cataline.
For, as it engaged only the city, or at moft a
province in Italy, a dictator invefted with that
unlimited authority which the laws conferred
on him, might eafily have diffipated that con-
fpiracy, which was with difficulty fuppreffed by
a numerous concurrence of fortunate circumftances ; which human prudence had no reafon
to expect.   Inftead of that, the Senate contented itfelf with committing all its power into
the hands of confuls ; whence it happened that
Cicero, in order to act effectually, was obliged
to exceed that power in a capital circumftance ;
and though the public, in their firft tranfports,
approved of his conduct, he was very juftly
called to an account afterwards for the blood he
had fpilt contrary to the laws ; a reproach they
could not not have made to a dictator.   But the
eloquence of the conful carried all before it ;
and preferring, though · a Roman, his own
glory to his country, he thought lefs of the
moft legal, and certain method of faving the
ftate, than the means of fecuring all the honour
of

of such a transaction to himself *.   Thus was he very justly honoured as the deliverer of Rome, and as justly punished as the violator of its laws. For, however honourable was his repeal, it was certainly a matter of favour.

After all, in whatever manner this important commission may be conferred, it is of consequence to limit its duration to a short term; which should on no occasion be prolonged.   In those conjunctures, when it is necessary to appoint a dictator, the state is presently saved or destroyed, which causes being over, the dictature becomes useless and tyrannical.   At Rome, the dictators held their office only for six months; and the greater part resigned before that term expired.   Had the time appointed been longer, it is to be apprehended they would have been tempted to make it longer still; as did the *decemvir* whose office lasted a whole year.   The dictator had no more time allotted him than was necessary to dispatch the business for which he was appointed; so that he had not leisure to think of other projects.

* This is what he could not be certain of, in proposing a dictator; not daring to nominate himself, and not being assured his colleague would do it.

C H A P. VII.

Of the Cenforfhip.

AS the declaration of the general will is made by the laws, fo the declaration of the public judgment is made by their cenfure. The public opinion is a kind of law, which the Cenfor puts in execution, in particular cafes, after the example of the prince.

So far, therefore, is the cenforial tribunal from being the arbiter of popular opinions, it only declares them ; and, whenever it departs from them, its decifions are vain and ineffectual.

It is ufelefs to diftinguifh the manners of a nation by the objects of its efteem; for thefe depend on the fame principle, and are neceffarily confounded together. Among all people in the world, it is not nature, but opinion, which determines the choice of their pleafures. Correct the prejudices and opinions of men, and their manners will correct themfelves. We always admire what is beautiful, or what appears fo ;

fo; but it is in our judgment we are miftaken;.
it is this judgment then. we are to regulate.
Whoever judges of manners, takes upon him
to judge of honour; and whoever judges of
honour, decides from opinion.

The opinions of a people depend on the conftitution; though the laws do not govern,
manners, it is the legiflature that gives rife to
them. As the legiflature grows feeble, manners,
degenerate, but the judgment of the cenfors.
will not then effect what the power of the.laws,
have not before effected.

It.follows, hence,.that.the office of a cenfor
may be ufeful to the prefervation of manners,
but never to their. re-eftablifhment. Eftablifh
cenfors. during the vigour of the.laws; when,
this is paft, all is over; no legal means can be
effectual when the laws have loft their force.

The cenfor is prefervative of manners, by
preventing the corruption of opinions, by maintaining their. morality and propriety by judicious applications, and.even fometimes by fettling
them when in a fluctuating fituation. The ufe

L 5.   of

of feconds in duels, though carried to the greateft excefs in France, was abolifhed by the following words inferted in one of the kings
edicts; *As to thofe who have the cowardice to call
themfelves feconds.* This judgment, anticipating
that of the public, was effectual and put an end
to that cuftom at once. But when the fame
edicts pronounced it cowardice to fight a duel;
though it is certainly true, yet as it was contrary to the popular opinion, the public laughed at a determination fo contrary to their own.

I have obferved elfewhere * that the public
opinion, being fubjected to no conftraint, there
fhould be no appearance of it in the tribunal
eftablifhed to reprefent it. One cannot too
much admire with what art this fpring of action,
entirely neglected among the moderns, was employed by the Romans, and ftill more effectually
by the Lacedemonians.

A man of bad morals, having made an excellent propofal in the council at Sparta, the

---

* I do but flightly mention here, what I have
treated more at large in my letter to M. d'Alembert.

Ephori,

Ephori, without taking any notice of it, caufed the fame propofal to be made by a citizen of character and virtue. How honourable was this proceeding to the one, and how difgraceful to the other; and that without directly praifing or blaming either! Some drunkards of Samos, having behaved indecently in the tribunal of the Ephori, it was the next day permitted, by a public edict, that the Samians might become flaves. Would an actual punifhment have been fo fevere as fuch impunity? When the Spartans had once paffed their judgment on the decency or propriety of any behaviour, all Greece fubmitted to their opinion.

C H A P. VIII.

Of political Religion.

IN the firft ages of the world, men had no other kings than gods, nor any other government than what was purely theocratical. It required a great alteration in their fentiments and ideas, before they could prevail on themfelves, to look upon a fellow creature as a mafter, and think it went well with them.

Hence,

Hence, a deity being constantly placed at the head of every political society, it followed that there was as many different gods as people. Two communities, personally strangers to each other, and almost always at variance, could not long acknowlege the same master; nor could two armies, drawn up against each other in battle, obey the same chief. Thus Polytheism became a natural consequence of the division of nations, and thence the want of civil and theological toleration, which are perfectly the same, as will be shewn hereafter.

The notion of the Greeks, in pretending to trace their own gods among those of the Barbarian nations, took its rise evidently from the ambition of being thought the natural sovereigns of those people. In this age, however, we think that a most absurd part of erudition, which relates to the identity of the deities of different nations, and according to which it is supposed that Moloch, Saturn and Chronos were one and the same god; and that the Baal of the Phenicians, the Zeus of the Greeks, and the Jupiter of the Latins were the same deity; as if any thing could be found in common

be-

between chimerical beings bearing different names !

If it be afked why there were no religious wars among the Pagans, when every ftate had thus its peculiar deity and worfhip ? I anfwer, it was plainly for this very reafon, that each ftate having its own peculiar religion as well as government, no diftinction was made between the obedience paid to their gods. and that due to their laws. Thus their political were at the fame time theological wars ; and the departments of their deities were prefcribed by the limits of their refpective nations. The god of one people had no authority over another people ; nor were thefe Pagan deities jealous of their prerogatives ; but divided the adoration of mankind amicably between them. ˙ Even Mofes himfelf fometimes fpeaks in the fame manner of the god of Ifrael. It is true the Hebrews defpifed the gods of the Canaanites, a people profcribed and devoted to deftruction, whofe poffeffions were given them for an inheritance : but they fpeak with more reverence of the deities of the neighbouring nations whom they were forbidden to attack. *Wilt thou not poffefs that,* fays Jeptha to Sihon, king of the Ammonites,

*nites, which Chemoth thy God giveth thee to pof-
fefs? So whomfoever the Lord our God fhall drive
out from before us, them will we poffefs.* There is
in this paffage, I think, an acknowleged fimili-
tude between the rights of Chemofh, and thofe
of the God of Ifrael.

· But when the Jews, being fubjefted to the
kings of Babylon, and afterwards to thofe of
Syria, perfifted in refufing to acknowlege any
god but their own, this refufal was efteemed
an aft of rebellion againft their conquerer, and
drew upon them thofe perfecutions we read of
in their hiftory, and of which no other example
is extant previous to the eftablifhment of chriftianity *.

The religion of every people being thus exclufively annexed to the laws of the ftate, the
only method of converting nations was to fubdue them ; warriors were the only miffionaries ;
and the obligation of changing their religion
being a law to the vanquifhed, they were firft
to be conquered before they were folicited on

* It is evident that the war of the Phocians, called
an holy war was not a religious war. Its objeft was
to punifh facrilege, and not to fubdue infidels.

this

this head. So far were men from fighting for the gods, that their gods, like thofe of Homer, fought in behalf of mankind. Each people demanded the victory from its refpective deity, and expreffed their gratitude for it by the erection of new altars. The Romans before they befieged any fortrefs fummoned its gods to abandon it; and though it be true they left the people of Tarentum in poffeffion of their angry deities, it is plain they looked upon thofe gods as fubjected and obliged to do homage to their own: They left the vanquifhed in poffeffion of their religion as they fometimes did in that of their laws; a wreathe for Jupiter of the Capitol, being often the only tribute they exacted.

At length, the Romans having extended their religion with their empire, and fometimes even adopted the deities of the vanquifhed, the people of this vaft empire found themfelves in poffeffion of a multiplicity of gods and religions; which not differing effentially from each other, Paganifm became infenfibly one and the fame religion throughout the world.

Things were in this ftate, when Jefus came to eftablifh his fpiritual kingdom on earth; a defign

fign which, neceffarily dividing the theological
from the political fyftem, gave rife to thofe inteftine divifions which have ever fince continued
to embroil the profeffion of Chriftianity. Now
this new idea of a kingdom in the other world,
having never entered into the head of the Pagans, they regarded the Chriftians as actual
rebels, who, under an hypocritical fhew of
humility, waited only a proper opportunity to
render themfelves independent, and artfully to
ufurp that authority, which in their weak and
infant ftate they pretended to refpect : and this
was undoubtedly the caufe of their being per-
fecuted.

What the Pagans were apprehenfive of, alfo,
did, in procefs of time, actually come to pafs.
Things put on a new face, and the meek Chriftians, as their number increafed, changed their
tone, while their invifible kingdom of the other
world, became, under a vifible head, the moft
defpotic and tyrannical in this.

As in all countries, however, there were civil governors, and laws, there refulted from
this two-fold power a perpetual ftruggle for
jurifdiction, which renders a perfect fyftem of
do-

domestic policy almost impossible in Christian
states; and prevents us from ever coming to a
determination, whether it be the prince or the
priest we are bound to obey.

Some nations indeed, even in Europe or its
neighbourhood, have endeavoured to preserve
or re-establish the ancient system, but without
success; the spirit of Christianity hath univer-
sally prevailed.   Religious worship hath always
remained, or again become independent of the
sovereign, and without any necessary connection
with the body of the state.   Mahomet had
very salutary and well-connected views in his
political system, and so long as his modes of
government subsisted under the caliphs and their
successors, that government remained perfectly
uniform, and so far good.   But the Arabians
becoming wealthy, learned, polite, indolent
and cowardly, were subdued by the Barbarians:
then the division between the two powers re-
commenced; and though it be less apparent
among the Mahometans than among Christians,
it is nevertheless to be distinguished, particularly in the sect of Ali: there are some states,
also, as in Persia, where this division is constantly perceptible.

Among

Among us, the kings of England are placed at the head of the church, as are also the Czars in Ruffia : but by this title they are not so properly masters as ministers of the religion of those countries : they are not possessed of the power to change it, but only to maintain its present form.   Wherever the Clergy constitute a collective body *, they will be both masters and legislators in their own cause.   There are therefore two sovereigns in England and Ruffia, as well as elsewhere.

Of all Christian authors, Mr. Hobbes was the only one who saw the evil and the remedy, and that hath ventured to propose the re-union

* It must be observed, that it is not so much the formal assemblies of the clergy, such as are held in France, which unite them together in a body, as the communion of their churches.   Communion and excommunication form the social compact of the clergy ; a compact by means of which they will always maintain their ascendency over both kings and people.   All the priests that communicate together are fellow-citizens, though they should be personally as distant, as the extremities of the world.   This invention is a master-piece in policy.   The Pagan priests had nothing like it ; and therefore never had any clerical body.

of the two heads of this eagle, and to reftore that political union, without which no ftate or government can be well conftituted. But he ought to have feen that the prevailing fpirit of Chriftianity was incompatible with his fyftem, and that the intereft of the Church would be always too powerful for the ftate. It was not fo much that which was really falfe and fhocking in the writings of this philofopher, as what was really juft and true, that rendered him odious *.

I conceive that, by a proper difplay of hiftorical facts, in this point of view, it would be eafy to refute the oppofite fentiments both of Bayle and Warburton; the former of which pretends that no religion whatever can be of fervice to the body politic, and the latter that Chriftianity is its beft and firmeft fupport. It might be proved againft the firft, that every

* In a letter of Grotius to his brother, dated the 11th of April, 1643, may be feen what that great Civilian approved and blamed in his book *de cive.* It is true that Grotius, being indulgent, feems inclined to forgive the author, the faults of his book, for the fake of its merits, the reft of the world, however, were not fo candid.

ftate

ftate in the world hath been founded on the
bafis of religion; and againft the fecond, that
the precepts of Chriftianity are at the bottom
more prejudicial than conducive to the ftrength
of the ftate.

In order to make myfelf fully underftood,
I need only give a little more precifion to the
vague ideas, generally entertained of political
religion.

Religion, confidered as it relates to fociety,
which is either general or particular, may be
diftinguifhed into two kinds, viz. the religion
of the man and that of the citizen. The firft,
deftitute of temples, altars, or rites, confined
purely to the internal worfhip of the fupreme
Being, and to the performance of the eternal
duties of morality, is the pure and fimple religion of the gofpel; this is genuine theifm,
and may be called the law of natural divinity.
The other, adopted only in one country, whofe
gods and tutelary faints are hence peculiar to itfelf, is compofed of certain dogmas, rites, and
external modes of worfhip prefcribed by the
laws of fuch country; all foreigners being accounted Infidels, Aliens and Barbarians; this
kind

kind of religion extends the duties and privileges of men no farther than to its own altars. Such were all the religions of primitive ages, to which may be given the name of the law of civil or pofitive divinity.

There is a third kind of religion ftill more extraordinary, which dividing fociety into two legiflatures, two chiefs, and two parties, fubjects mankind to contradictory obligations, and prevents them from being at once devotees and citizens. Such is the religion of the Lamas, of the Japanefe, and of the Roman Catholics; which may be denominated the religion of the priefts, and is productive of a fort of mixed and unfociable obligation, for which we have no name.

If we examine thefe three kinds of religion in a political light, they have all their faults. The third is fo palpably defective that it would be mere lofs of time, to point them out. Whatever contributes to diffolve the focial union is good for nothing: all inftitutions which fet man in contradiction with himfelf are of no ufe.

The

The fecond is fo far commendable as it unites
divine worfhip with a refpect for the laws, and
that, making the country the object of the people's adoration, the citizen is taught that to ferve
the ftate is to ferve its tutelary divinity.   This
is a fpecies of theocracy, in which there fhould
be no other pontiff than the prince, no other
priefts than the magiftrates.   To die, in fuch
a ftate, for their country, is to fuffer martyrdom ;
to violate the laws is impiety ; and to doom a
criminal to public execration is to devote him
to the anger of the gods.

It is blameable, however, in that, being
founded on falfehood and deceit, it leads mankind into error ; rendering them credulous and
fuperftitious, it fubftitutes vain ceremonies inftead of the true worfhip of the deity.   It is
further blameable, in that, becoming exclufive
and tyrannical, it makes people fanguinary and
perfecuting ; fo that a nation fhall fometimes
breathe nothing but murder and maffacre, and
think, at the fame time, they are doing an holy
action in cutting the throats of thofe who worfhip the gods in a different manner from themfelves.   This circumftance places fuch a people
in

in a natural ſtate of war with all others, which is very unfavourable to their own ſafety.

There remains then only the rational and manly religion of Chriſtianity; not however, as it is profeſſed in modern times, but as it is diſplayed in the goſpel, which is quite another thing. According to this holy, ſublime, and true religion, mankind, being all the children of the ſame God, acknowlege themſelves to be brothers, and the ſociety which unites them diſ- ſolves only in death.

But this religion, having no particular rela- tion to the body politic, leaves the laws in poſ- ſeſſion only of their own force, without adding any thing to it; by which means the firmeſt bonds of ſuch particular ſociety are of no ef- fect. Add to this, that Chriſtianity is ſo far from attaching the hearts of the citizens to the ſtate, that it detaches them from it, as well as from all worldly objects in general : than which nothing can be more contrary to the ſpirit of ſociety.

It is ſaid that a nation of true Chriſtians would form the moſt perfect ſociety imaginable.
To

To this affertion, however, there is one great objection; and this is, that a fociety of true Chriftians would not be a fociety of men. Nay, I will go fo far as to affirm, that this fuppofed fociety, with all its perfection, would neither be of the greateft ftrength nor duration. In confequence of its being perfect, it would want the ftrongeft ties of connexion; and thus this very circumftance would deftroy it.

Individuals might do their duty, the people might be obedient to the laws, the chiefs might be juft, the magiftrate incorrupt, the foldiery might look upon death with contempt, and there might prevail neither vanity nor luxury, in fuch a ftate. So far all would go well; but let us look farther.

Chriftianity is a fpiritual religion, relative only to celeftial objects: the Chriftian's inheritance, is not of this world. He performs his duty, it is true, but this he does with a profound indifference for the good or ill fuccefs of his endeavours. Provided he hath nothing to reproach himfelf with, it is of little importance to him whether matters go well or ill here below·

low. If the ftate be in a flourifhing fituation, he can hardly venture to rejoice in the public felicity, left he fhould be puffed up with the inordinate pride of his country's glory; if the ftate decline, he bleffes the hand of God that humbles his people to the duft.

It is farther neceffary to the peace and harmony of fociety, that all the citizens fhould be without exception equally good Chriftians; for, if unhappily there fhould be one of them ambitious or hypocritical, if there fhould be found among them a Cataline or a Cromwell, it is certain he would make an eafy prey of his pious countrymen. Chriftian charity doth not eafily permit the thinking evil of one's neighbour. No fooner fhould an individual difcover the art of impofing on the majority, and be invefted with fome portion of public authority, than he would become a dignitary. Chriftians muft not fpeak evil of dignities; thus refpected, he would thence affume power; Chriftians muft obey the fuperior powers. Does the depofitary of power abufe it? he becomes the rod by which it pleafes God to chaftife his children.

'M   And

And, would their confciences permit them to drive out the ufurper, the public tranquillity muft be broken, and violence and blood-fhed fucceed; all this agrees but ill with the meeknefs of true Chriftians; and, after all, what is it to them, whether they are freemen or flaves in this vale of mifery? Their effential concern is to work out their falvation, and obtain happinefs in another world; to effect which, their refignation in this, is held to be their duty.

Should fuch a ftate be forced into a war with any neighbouring power? The citizens might march readily to the combat, without thinking of flight; they might do their duty in the field, but they would have no ardour for victory; being better inftructed to die than to conquer. Of what confequence is it to them, whether they are victors or vanquifhed? Think what advantages an impetuous and fanguine enemy might take of their ftoicifm! draw them out againft a brave and generous people, ardently infpired with the love of glory and their country; fuppofe, for inftance, your truly Chriftian republic againft that of Sparta or of Rome; what would be the confequence? Your

3   de-

devout Chriftians would be beaten, difcomfited and knocked on the head, before they had time to look about them ; their only fecurity depending on the contempt which their enemy might entertain for them. It was, in my opinion, a fine oath that was taken by the foldiers of Fabius. They did not make a vow either to die or conquer ; they fwore they would return conquerors, and punctually performed their oath. Chriftian troops could not have made fuch a vow, they would have been afraid of tempting the Lord their God.

But I am all this while committing a blunder, in fpeaking of a Chriftian republic ; one of thefe terms neceffarily excluding the other. Chriftianity inculcates fervitude and dependence ; the fpirit of it is too favourable to tyrants, for them not fometimes to profit by it. True Chriftians are formed for flaves ; they know it, and never trouble themfelves about confpiracies and infurrections ; this tranfitory life is of too little value in their efteem.

Will it be faid, the Chriftians are excellent foldiers ? I deny it. Produce me your Chriftian

ſtian troops. For my part, I know of no true
Chriſtian ſoldiers. Do you name thoſe of the
Cruſades? I anſwer, that, not to call in queſtion
the valour of the Cruſaders, they were very
far from being Chriſtian citizens: they were
the ſoldiers of the prieſt, the citizens of the
church; they fought for its ſpiritual country,
which ſome how or other, it had converted into
a temporal one. To ſet this matter in the beſt
light, it was a kind of return to Paganiſm; for
as the goſpel did not eſtabliſh any national religion, an holy war could not poſſibly be carried
on by true Chriſtians.

Under the Pagan emperors, the Chriſtian ſoldiers were brave; of this all the Chriſtian writers aſſure us, and I believe them; the motive of their bravery was a ſpirit of honour or
emulation, excited by the Pagan troops. But
when the emperors became Chriſtians, this motive of emulation no longer ſubſiſted; and when
the Croſs had put the Eagle to flight, the
Roman valour diſappeared.

But, laying aſide political conſiderations, let
us return to the matter of right, and aſcertain
its

its true principles with regard to this important point. The right which the focial compact confers on the fovereign, extending no farther than to public utility *, the fubject is not accountable to that fovereign, on account of any opinions he may entertain, that have nothing to do with the community. Now, it is of great importance to a ftate, that every citizen fhould be of a religion that may infpire him with a regard for his duty; but the tenets of that religion are no farther interefting to the community than as they relate to morals, and to the difcharge of thofe obligations, which the profeffor lies under to his fellow citizens. If we

---

* _In a republic_, fays the Marquis d'A. _every one is perfectly at liberty, becaufe no one may injure another._ This is the invariable limit of republican liberty, nor is it poffible to ftate the cafe more precifely. I cannot deny myfelf the pleafure of fometimes quoting this manufcript, though unknown to the public, in order to do honour to the memory of an illuftrious and refpectable perfonage, who preferved the integrity of the citizen even in the miniftry, and adopted the moft unpright and falutary views in the government of his country.

except

except thefe, the individual may profefs what others he pleafes, without the fovereign's having any right to interfere; for, having no jurifdiction in the other world, it is nothing to the fovereign, what becomes of the citizens in a future life, provided they difcharge the duties incumbent on them in the prefent.

There is a profeffion of Faith, therefore, purely political; the articles of which it is in the province of the fovereign to afcertain, not precifely as articles of religion, but as the fentiments due to fociety, without which it is impoffible to be a good citizen or faithful fubject *. Without compelling any one to adopt thefe fentiments, the fovereign may alfo equitably banifh him the fociety; not indeed as impious, but as unfociable, as incapable of having a fincere re-

* Cæfar, in pleading for Cataline, endeavoured to eftablifh the doctrine of the Mortality of the Soul: Cato and Cicero, in anfwer to him, did not enter into a philofophical difcuffion of the argument, but contented themfelves with fhewing that Cæfar had fpoken like a bad citizen, and advanced a dogma pernicious to the ftate. And this was in fact the point only that come before the Senate of Rome, and not a queftion in theology.

gard

gard to juſtice, and of ſacrificing his life, if required, to his duty.   Again, ſhould any one,
after having made a public profeſſion of ſuch
ſentiments, betray his diſbelief of them by his
miſconduct, he may equitably be puniſhed with
death ; having committed the greateſt of all
crimes, that of belying his heart in the face of
the laws.

The tenets of political religion ſhould be few
and ſimple ; they ſhould be laid down alſo wit
preciſion, and without explication or comment.
The exiſtence of a powerful, intelligent, bene-
ficent, preſcient and provident Deity ; a future
ſtate ; the reward of the virtuous and the puniſhment of the wicked ; the ſacred nature of
the ſocial contract, and of the laws ; theſe
ſhould be its poſitive tenets.   As to thoſe of a
negative kind I would confine myſelf ſolely to
one, by forbidding perſecution.

Thoſe who affect to make a diſtinction between civil and religious toleration, are, in my
opinion miſtaken.   It is impoſſible to live cor-
dially in peace with thoſe whom we firmly believe devoted to damnation : to love them would
be to hate the Deity for puniſhing them, it is
therefore abſolutely neceſſary for us either to
per-

perfecute or to convert them. Wherever the
fpirit of religious perfecution fubfifts, it is impoffible it fhould not have fome effect on the
civil police, in which cafe, the fovereign is no
longer fovereign even in a fecular view; the priefts
become the real mafters, and kings only their
officers.

In modern governments, where it is impoffible to fupport an exclufive national religion, it
is requifite to tolerate all fuch, as breathe the
fpirit of toleration toward others, provided their
tenets are not contradictory to the duty of a good
citizen. But whofoever fhould prefume to fay,
There is no falvation out of the pale of our church,
ought to be banifhed the ftate; unlefs indeed
the ftate be an ecclefiaftical one, and the prince
a pontiff. Such a dogma is of ufe only in a
theocratical government; in every other it is deftructive. The reafon which it is faid Henry
IV. gave, for embracing the Roman Catholic religion, ought to have made an honeft man reject
it, and more particularly a prince capable of
reafoning on the fubject.

C H A P.

CHAP. IX.

The Conclusion.

HAVING thus stated the true principles of politic law, and endeavoured to fix the state on its proper basis, it remains to shew in what manner it is supported by external relations.

Under this head would be comprehended, the laws of nations and commerce, the laws of war and conquest, leagues, negotiations, treaties, &c. But these present a new prospect, too vast and extensive for so short a sight as mine; which should be confined to objects less distant and more adapted to my limited capacity.

FINIS.

In the Prefs, and fpeedily will be publifhed,

T H E

MISCELLANEOUS WORKS

O F

Mr. J. J. R O U S S E A U.

Alfo,

A   N E W   E D I T I O N,

Revifed and Corrected from the Author's laft
corrected Copy. In 4 Volumes.

E   L   O   I   S   A:

O R,   A

Series of Original Letters between two Lovers.

By Mr. J. J. R O U S S E A U.

NEW BOOKS,

Printed for T. BECKET and P. A. DE HONDT, in the Strand.

1. Lady M. W. M—e's Letters, 3 Vol. 12mo.
2. Clark's Letters on the Spanish Nation, 4to.
3. King of Pruſſia's Campaigns. 12mo.
4. Effuſions of Friendſhip and Fancy, 2 Vol. 12mo.
5. The Letters that paſſed between Theodoſius and Conſtantia. 12mo.
6. Hiſtory of Louiſiana, 2 Vol. 12mo.
7. Death of Adam. 12mo.
8. Fingal, an ancient Epic Poem, 4to.
9. Temora, an ancient Epic Poem, 4to.
10. A critical Diſſertation on the Poems of Oſſian, 4to.

Speedily will be publiſhed,

1. MORAL TALES.

In Two pocket Volumes.

By Mr. MARMONTEL.

2: The LOVES of

CHÆREAS and CALLIRRHOE.

In Two pocket Volumes.